Bridging 2 to 3

Summer SPLASH

LEARNING ACTIVITIES

Brighter Child®
An imprint of Carson-Dellosa Publishing LLC
Greensboro, North Carolina

Brighter Child®
An imprint of Carson-Dellosa Publishing LLC
P.O. Box 35665
Greensboro, NC 27425 USA

Printed in the USA • All rights reserved.   ISBN 978-1-60996-969-1

03-137131151

Table of Contents

Making the Most of
Summer Splash Learning Activities

This resource contains a myriad of fun and challenging reading and math activities. The reading pages provide practice in synonyms and antonyms, fact and opinion, making inferences, and drawing conclusions. The math pages review skills taught in second grade, such as addition and subtraction, multiplication and division, and basic geometry.

Most of the activities in the book are designed so that your child can work independently. However, your child will enjoy the activities much more if you work alongside him or her. Make sure to let your child know that this is not a workbook with tests, but a book of fun activities that you can do together. The book is divided into 10 weeks, with about eight activity pages per week. Feel free to choose how many per day and in which order you do the activities, but complete the weeks in sequence, since activities become increasingly challenging as the book progresses.

Summer Splash Learning Activities provides an important link between your child's second- and third-grade school years. It reviews what your child learned in second grade, providing the confidence and skills that he or she needs for the coming fall. The activities in this book will help your child successfully bridge the gap between second and third grade by reviewing and reinforcing the important and essential skills for his or her continued academic success. These activities are designed to

- review skills in math, reading, and language arts that your child learned the previous year.

- give you an opportunity to monitor your child's skills in various areas.

- offer you a chance to spend special time with your child.

- enable your child to continue routine daily learning activities.

- give you a chance to praise your child's efforts.

- demonstrate to your child that you value lifetime learning.

- make you an active and important part of your child's educational development.

Getting Started

In order for your child to get the most from the activities in this resource, use these helpful tips to make these learning experiences interesting and, most of all, fun!

- Set aside a time each day for completing the activities. Make it a time when your child will be most ready to learn, and make it a routine.
- Provide a pleasant, quiet place to work. This means no TV in your child's work area. Also, make sure there is a sufficient light source.
- Review in advance the activity page(s) your child will complete that session. This way, you will be able to familiarize yourself with the lesson.
- Have your child read the directions aloud beforehand to make sure he or she understands the activity. Instructions are written for the child, but he or she may need your help reading and/or understanding them.
- Let your child help choose which activity he or she would like to complete that day.
- Praise all your child's work. It's the effort, not necessarily the end result, that counts most.

No one knows better than you how your child learns best, so use this book to enhance the way you already work with him or her. Use every opportunity possible as a learning experience, whether making a trip through the grocery store or riding in the car. Pose problems and let your child figure out how to solve them, asking questions such as *Which route should we take to the park? What could we use to make a plant grow straight?* or *How high should we hang this shelf?* Also, respond excitedly to discoveries your child makes throughout the day with comments such as *That rock is really unique! I wonder how long it took the spider to spin that web;* or *You spent your money wisely.* In this way, you will encourage and motivate your child to learn throughout the day and for the rest of his or her life, providing the confidence and self-esteem he or she needs for continued academic success.

Everyday Learning Activities

Use these simple educational activities to keep your child's mind engaged and active during the summer months and all year long!

- Ask your child to make a schedule of events for the day, in the order in which they will take place. Ask him or her to prioritize the list and number the events.

- On a neighborhood walk or while driving in the car, encourage your child to read all the street signs and numbers.

- Read with your child each day. Encourage your child to retell the story to you. Then, have him or her make up original adventures for the story characters or write an additional chapter.

- Have your child write down important dates such as family birthdays, important trips or outings, or holidays. Be sure your child capitalizes the name of the month and week and uses a comma between the day and year.

- During a visit to the park or playground, invite your child to describe what he or she sees there, using as many adjectives as possible.

- Have your child list three things you can smell, feel, taste, or see in a particular room of the house or on a "senses walk."

- Have your child identify as many parts of the human body as he or she can. Ask him or her to describe the function of each part, if possible.

- Ask your child to read a recipe with you for a simple dish. Practice measuring skills by simulating measuring out the ingredients with water or rice in measuring spoons or cups.

- Have your child read the price of items in a store or supermarket. Challenge him or her to estimate how much can be bought with a designated amount of money. Can your child figure out how much change is left over?

- Encourage your child to tell you whether certain objects in your home (sofa, pencil) would be measured in pounds or ounces.

- Fill a measuring cup with water to different levels, and invite your child to read the measurement and then write it as a fraction.

- Encourage your child to read nonfiction library books and make up creative stories about the subject matter (e.g., lions or airplanes).

Assessment

1. Circle the word that means the same as the underlined word.

The <u>swift</u> rabbit escaped from the chasing fox.

A. slow   **B.** baby

C. quick   **D.** furry

2. Circle the word that means the opposite of the underlined word.

Mom gave me an extra dollar in my allowance because my room looked <u>immaculate</u>.

A. clean   **B.** tidy

C. messy   **D.** funny

3. In which sentence does the underlined word have the same meaning as the underlined word in the sentence below?

My teacher asked us to take out a <u>sheet</u> of paper.

A. The roads have become a <u>sheet</u> of ice.

B. The nurse wrapped a <u>sheet</u> around the sleeping baby.

C. Have you seen my <u>sheet</u> of homework assignments?

D. We used an old <u>sheet</u> as the roof for our fort.

4. Which sentence is a fact?

A. Saturn is the coolest planet because it has rings.

B. Life does not exist on Earth.

C. Jupiter is the largest planet.

D. Mars is the most interesting planet because of its color.

5. Circle the letter of the word that does not belong.

A. pig   **B.** horse

C. barn   **D.** sheep

6. What is found at the end of informational books?

A. Title page   **B.** Index

C. Table of contents   **D.** Dictionary entry

Assessment

7. Which conclusion best fits the sentence below?

Brenda grabbed a bagel from the refrigerator, threw her backpack over her shoulder, and ran for the bus.

   A. She is late for school.   **B.** She is mad at someone.

   C. She already ate.   **D.** She has to feed the dog.

8. Your teacher asks you to write a poem about your birthday party. What might you name it?

   A. Pizza Party   **B.** Decorating with Balloons

   C. Best Friends   **D.** My Surprise Party

9. Which of these happens first?

   A. Soon, I will walk to the library.

   B. Eventually, I will go to the store.

   C. First, I need to go to school.

   D. Someday, I will go to the football game.

10. Using the information given, which sentence is not a logical inference?

When Westin got home, he found that the bird's nest was empty.

   A. The eggs hatched, and the birds flew away.

   B. The eggs were stolen by a nest-robbing dinosaur.

   C. The eggs were eaten by a snake.

   D. The eggs were blown out of the nest in a thunderstorm.

11. Write two similarities and two differences between yourself and a family member.

Similarities:

1. _I like sports_

2. _My brother likes sports_

Differences:

1. _I'm nine years old_

2. _He's ten years old_

8

Assessment

Read each passage and answer the questions.

12. What was Jason's job?

Jason heard the garbage truck coming and remembered that his job wasn't done yet.

A. to deliver newspapers   B. to walk the dog

C. to water the plants   **D. to take out the trash**

13. What will probably happen next in the story?

A. Jason ran toward the garage and quickly wheeled the trash cans outside.

B. Jason waved to the garbage truck driver.

C. Jason went back to reading his book.

D. Jason went downstairs to finish the dishes.

14. How do you think Jenny is feeling?

Jenny threw herself on her bed and buried her head in a pillow.

A. proud   **B. sad**

C. cheerful   D. clever

15. What was the cause of Mom spilling her coffee?

The cat jumped into Mom's lap and she spilled her coffee.

A. Mom is clumsy.

B. The cat tripped Mom.

C. The cat jumped into Mom's lap.

D. Mom was mad at the cat.

16. Where did the sister leave her math book?

My sister always forgets things. Last week, she left her math book at our grandmother's house. Yesterday, she left her lunch at home. Today, she left her field trip money. Who knows what she will forget tomorrow?

A. home   **B. school**

C. her friend's house   D. her grandmother's house

Assessment Analysis

Answer Key:

1. C. *A*		9.	C.
2. C. *B*		10.	B.
3. C. *C*		11.	Answers will vary.
4. C. *C*		12.	D. *A*
5. C. *C*		13.	A. *B*
6. B. *D*		14.	B. *C*
7. A.		15.	C. *D*
8. D.		16.	D. *D*

After reviewing the assessment, match the problems answered incorrectly to the corresponding activity pages. Your child should spend extra time on those activities to strengthen his or her reading skills.

Number	Skill	Activity Page(s)
1.	synonyms	14–15
2.	antonyms	16–17
3.	homonyms	22–23
4.	fact or opinion	24–25
5.	classification	30–31
6., 12.	drawing conclusions	38–41
7.	main idea	32–33
8.	parts of a book	46–49
9.	sequencing	54–55
10.	making inferences	62–65
11.	compare and contrast	56–57
13.	predicting outcomes	70–73
14.	character analysis	78–79
15.	cause and effect	80–81
16.	reading for details	86–89

8

Assessment

Write each numeral.

1. seven _7_   nineteen _19_   thirty-seven _37_

    seventy _70_   sixty-five _65_

What is the value of:

2. 6 in 612? _hundred_   4 in 241? _ten_   9 in 9,243? _thousand_

3. 342 equals _300_ hundreds _40_ tens _2_ ones

4. 819 equals _800_ hundreds _1_ tens _9_ ones

5. 2,345 equals _2_ thousands _3_ hundreds _4_ tens _5_ ones

Use <, >, or = to compare the numerals.

6. 35 _<_ 71   10 _>_ 3   91 _<_ 94   68 _<_ 88

Solve the problems.

7.
```
  21        64        86        59        73
+ 42      + 12      + 11      + 19      + 17
 63        76        47         9        90
```

8.
```
  49        83        77        40        54
- 37      - 13      - 41      - 16      - 27
 12        70        36        24        27
```

9.
```
  12         7        79         8        32
x  2       x 6       x 7       x 2       x 8
 24        42       553        16       256
```

10.
```
7)49      5)35      4)28      6)38      8)25
  7         7                              
```

Assessment

Write the equations for each fact family.

11. 2, 4, 8

2 x 2 = 4
4 x 2 = 8
8 ÷ 2 = 4
8 ÷ 4 = 2

12. 5, 6, 30

5 x 6 = 30
6 x 5 = 30
30 ÷ 5 = 6
30 ÷ 6 = 5

Write the time shown on each clock.

13.

4 : 38

8 : 26

Count the money. Write how much.

14.

$7.36¢

Write the fractions. Then, use <, >, or = to compare.

15.

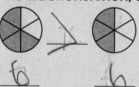

6   6

16.

8   8

Write the name of each shape.

17.

trapizaid   cilender   rhombus   circle

Solve each problem.

18. The soccer team scored 6 goals each game. They played 3 games. How many goals did they score? __18__ goals

19. Sam's family has 12 cookies. There are 4 people in Sam's family. How many cookies will each person get? __3__ cookies

Math Assessment

Assessment Analysis

Answer Key:

1. 7, 19, 37, 70, 65
2. 600, 40, 9,000
3. 3, 4, 2
4. 8, 1, 9
5. 2, 3, 4, 5 ✓
6. <, >, <, < ✓
7. 63, 76, 97, 78, 90
8. 12, 70, 36, 24, 27
9. 24, 42, 553, 16, 256

10. 7, 7, 7, 6 r2, 3 r1
11. Answers may be in a different order.
    $2 \times 4 = 8, 4 \times 2 = 8,$
    $8 \div 4 = 2, 8 \div 2 = 4$
12. Answers may be in a different order.
    $5 \times 6 = 30, 6 \times 5 = 30,$
    $30 \div 6 = 5, 30 \div 5 = 6$

13. 4:35, 8:26
14. $7.77
15. $\frac{4}{6} > \frac{3}{6}$
16. $\frac{4}{8} = \frac{4}{8}$
17. trapezoid, cylinder, parallelogram, circle
18. 18 goals
19. 3 cookies

After reviewing the assessment, match the problems answered incorrectly to the corresponding activity pages. Your child should spend extra time on those activities to strengthen his or her math skills.

Number	Skill	Activity Page(s)
1., 2., 3., 4., 5., 6.	numeration	18–21, 26–29
7., 8.	addition and subtraction	34–37, 42–45
9., 10., 11., 12.	multiplication and division	50–53, 58–61
13., 14.	time and money	66–69
15., 16.	fractions and decimals	74–77
17.	geometry	82–85
18., 19.	problem solving	90–92

The Great Word Race

Synonyms are words that have almost the same meaning.
Example: complete, finish

Find a synonym on the racetrack for each word below. Write the number of each word from the list next to the matching word on the racetrack. Be sure to work in order to move the race cars forward. Circle the car that wins the Great Word Race!

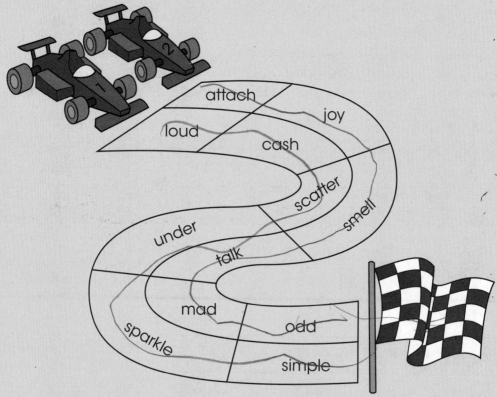

1. connect
2. noisy
3. money
4. happiness
5. spread
6. beneath
7. scent
8. speak
9. angry
10. glitter
11. strange

The Same Meaning

Complete the puzzle by finding the synonym of the bold word.
Use the words in the word bank.

| remember | ~~smart~~ | doctor | great |
| ~~grabbed~~ | starving | crowd | ~~bite~~ |

Down

1. My mom took me to our **physician** when I got sick.

2. My dog is so **intelligent** that he learned three new tricks in one day.

3. There was a huge **mob** of fans outside the concert.

4. My aunt **grasped** the railing as she came down the stairs.

5. Jack's puppy likes to **gnaw** on his bone.

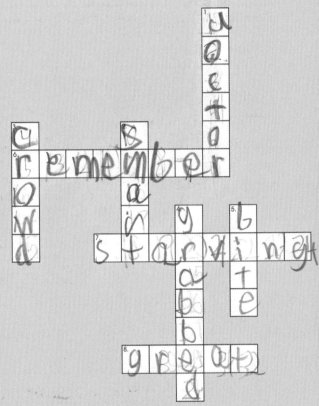

Across

6. Do you **recall** the phone number?

7. I ate two plates of spaghetti because I was **famished**.

8. Your birthday party was **superb**!

15

Opposite Meanings

> **Antonyms** are words with opposite meanings.
> **Example:** raise, lower

Read each word below. Then, find its antonym in the word bank and write it in the boxes. To find the answer to the riddle, read the letters in the bold boxes.

adult ~~brave~~ remember silent ~~cheap~~ filthy
~~whole~~ ~~begin~~ dangerous ~~stretch~~ ~~playful~~ catch

expensive: c h e a p
part: w h a l e
noisy: s i l e n t
clean: f i l t h y
toss: c a t c h
safe: d a n g e r o u s
end: b e g i n

shrink: s t r e t c h
child: a d u l t
scared: b r a v e
forget: r e m e m b e r
serious: p l a y f u l

What travels all around the world, yet always stays in the corner?

A P O S T A G E S T A M P !

16

Hot Air Antonyms

Find the antonym in the word bank for each bold word. Write the letter for each antonym on the matching balloon basket.

A. lower   **E.** scatter
B. simple   **F.** fresh
C. begin   **G.** tidy
D. dull

1. I watched the squirrel **collect** nuts before the snowstorm hit.

scatter

2. This bread must be old. It tastes **stale**.

fresh

3. I wish that I had studied more. The test was **difficult** for me.

simple

4. Painting is fun, but it can be **messy** at times.

tidy

5. Before the game, they always **raise** the flag.

lower

6. Did they **complete** their work?

begin

7. The stars are **bright** in the sky tonight.

dull

17

Naming Numbers in Word Form

Numbers can be written as words, as well as numerals. Below are the words for the numerals 0 through 12.

0–zero	1–one	2–two	3–three	4–four
5–five	6–six	7–seven	8–eight	9–nine
10–ten	11–eleven	12–twelve		

Study the word names above. Then, find the written name for each numeral. Use the matching letters to answer the question.

Where does the male emperor penguin keep the eggs warm?

73 18   45 92 35
74 19   46 93 36

20 51 75 61 __
21 52 76 62 85

ninety-three 93 I	sixty-two 62 T	forty-six 46 H
fifty-nine 59 R	seventy-four 74 O	fifty-two 52 E
nineteen 19 N	eighty-five 85 !	twenty-one 21 F
seventy-six 76 E	thirty-six 36 S	ninety 90 V

18

Naming Larger Numbers in Word Form

You can use **place value** columns to help you write numbers in word form. They look like this:

H	T	O
6	4	1

= six hundred forty-one

Th	H	T	O
3	2	1	8

= three thousand two hundred eighteen

Study the examples above. Then, read each number's name in word form. Color its matching number on the chicken or on the egg.

1. six thousand nine hundred eleven
2. four thousand seventy-three
3. nine thousand two hundred seven
4. eight hundred thirty-nine
5. nine thousand six hundred one
6. eight thousand three hundred ninety
7. four hundred seventeen
8. five thousand eighty-two
9. four hundred seventy
10. three thousand five hundred twelve
11. six thousand nine hundred fourteen

417 9,207 839

3,512 6,911 6,914

9,601 4,073 5,082

470 4,413 8,390

12. What numeral is left over? _____

Place Value

> 1 thousand, 2 hundreds, 3 tens, 2 ones
> is equal to the number 1,232. We say
> "one thousand two hundred thirty-two."
>
> __1__ thousand __2__ hundreds __3__ tens
> __2__ ones = __1,232__

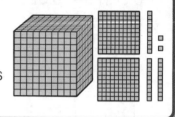

Study the example above. Then, write how many thousands, hundreds, tens, and ones. Write the total.

1.

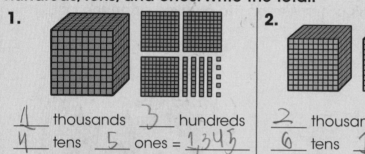

__1__ thousands __3__ hundreds
__4__ tens __5__ ones = __1,345__

2.

__2__ thousands __1__ hundreds
__6__ tens __1__ ones = __2,161__

3.

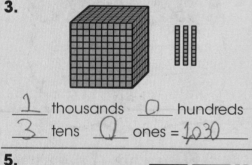

__1__ thousands __0__ hundreds
__3__ tens __0__ ones = __1,030__

4.

__3__ thousands __1__ hundreds
__0__ tens __0__ ones = __3,100__

5.

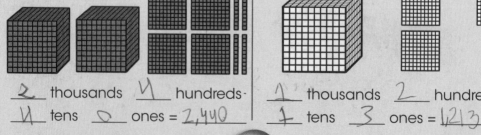

__2__ thousands __4__ hundreds
__4__ tens __0__ ones = __2,440__

6.

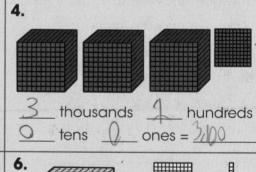

__1__ thousands __2__ hundreds
__1__ tens __3__ ones = __1,213__

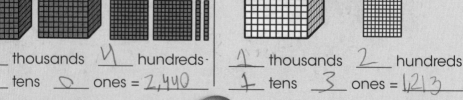
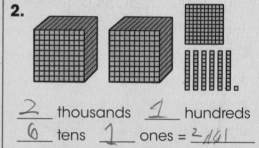

Place Value Practice

Study the example on page 20. Then, write the number of ten thousands, thousands, hundreds, tens, and ones in each numeral below.

		Ten Thousands	Thousands	Hundreds	Tens	Ones
1.	5,739	5	5	7	3	9
2.	14,650	1	4	6	5	0
3.	27,381	2	7	3	8	1
4.	40,736	4	0	7	3	6
5.	91,475	9	1	4	7	5
6.	55,837	5	5	8	3	7
7.	86,902	8	6	9	0	2
8.	4,560		4	5	6	0
9.	31,048	3	1	0	4	8
10.	11,111	1	1	1	1	1
11.	79,277	7	9	2	7	7
12.	68,593	6	8	5	9	3
13.	99,999	9	9	9	9	9
14.	48,305	4	8	3	0	5

What place value does each circled numeral represent?

15. 3,④56   hundred   90,②86   hundred

16. ⑦,394   thousand   ④7,519   ten thousand

17. ①6,321   ten thousand   38,1②7   tens

18. 25,0④7   tens   ⑧4,031   ten thousand

19. 39,⑤86   hundred   7②,797   thousand

20. 58,72⑨   ones   59,3⑥8   tens

21. 40,3⑦0   tens   30,58④   ones

22. ⑦2,532   ten thousand   ⑧6,395   ten thousand

23. 9⑥,411   thousand   39,⑤86   hundred

Many Meanings

Some words have more than one meaning. These words are called **homonyms.** You can tell which meaning is being used from the context clues of the sentence.

Write the homonym from the word bank that makes sense with the context clues in each pair of sentences.

~~tire~~ ~~break~~ ~~mean~~ straw ~~land~~ glasses book ~~free~~

1. Be careful not to ___break___ Mom's favorite vase.
   Should we take a ___break___ from practice to eat lunch?

2. Mom will ___glasses___ an appointment for Monday.
   Have you read the new ___glasses___ by that author?

3. What do you ___mean___ by that?
   The dog that lives next door is ___mean___, so let's stay away.

4. My cat is so old that chasing a mouse will ___tire___ her out.
   We got a flat ___tire___ when we drove to Florida.

5. The plane is due to ___land___ at 6:00 tonight.
   The large areas of ___land___ on Earth are called continents.

6. The zookeeper lifted the door to ___free___ the bird.
   I can't believe we read enough books to earn ___free___ pizza!

7. After you finish, set your lemonade ___straw___ on the counter.
   I am going to get new ___straw___ to help me see the board.

8. The farmer keeps ___book___ in the barn during the winter.
   Can you hand me a ___book___ for my milk shake?

More Than One Meaning

A **dictionary** will help you discover the multiple meanings of a word.

The words below are homonyms. Write two sentences that use different meanings for each word.

park

1. _play ground_
   stor
2. _scool_
   creep

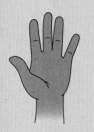

hand

3. _pawm_
   finger
4. _wrist_

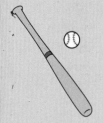

bat

5. _baseball_
   bat
6. _balle_
   base

Sea Horses

Read the passage below.

Sea horses are interesting creatures for many reasons. Their scientific name is *Hippocampus*. It comes from two Greek words: *hippos*, which means "horse" and *kampos*, which means "sea monster." To survive in the ocean, sea horses live in environments that camouflage them from predators. Sea horses range in size from 6 to 12 inches, although most are about 6 inches long. They can be many colors, including white, yellow, red, brown, black, and gray, with spots or stripes. However, the most interesting thing about sea horses is that they put a twist in parenting. Instead of females carrying the young, males carry them!

A male sea horse has a pouch on his underside where he carries eggs. The female sea horse places her eggs into the male's pouch. Then, the male sea horse carries the eggs for about 21 days until they hatch. The female sea horse visits the male sea horse every morning until the babies are born. Newborn sea horses rise to the surface of the water and take a gulp of air, which helps them stay upright.

When sea horses are born, they feed on tiny sea creatures, using their snouts. They are able to swim, but sometimes they get washed up onshore by storms or eaten by fish, crabs, or water birds.

A few days after giving birth, the male joins the female again. Within hours, he has a new sack full of eggs. This is the life cycle of the sea horse. Sea horses are indeed interesting animals!

Sea Horses

After reading "Sea Horses," answer the following questions.

1. What do newborn sea horses usually eat?

   A. crabs   **C.** tiny sea animals

   B. flowers   **D.** sand

2. Why do you think the author used the word *twist* in the first paragraph?

   _____

   _____

3. Why do newborn sea horses rise to the surface of the water?

   _____

   _____

4. What word means "sea monster"?

   A. kampos   **C.** hippos

   B. phylum   **D.** genus

5. In your opinion, what is the most interesting thing about the sea horse?

   _____

   _____

   _____

   _____

Writing in Expanded Form

The place value system is based on **groups of ten**. This chart shows how the thousands, hundreds, tens, and ones relate to each other.

1,000	100	10	1
1 thousand = 10 hundreds	1 hundred = 10 tens	1 ten = 10 ones	

This chart is helpful when writing numbers in expanded form.
$$3,649 = 3,000 + 600 + 40 + 9$$

Study the example above. Then, write each number in expanded form.

		Thousands	Hundreds	Tens	Ones
1.	9,516 =	9,000	+ 500	+ 10	+ 6
2.	2,358 =	2,000	+ 300	+ 50	+ 8
3.	1,407 =	1,000	+ 400	+ 0	+ 7
4.	921 =	0	+ 9	+ 2	+ 1
5.	7,800 =	7,000	+ 800	+ 0	+ 0
6.	3,264 =	3,000	+ 200	+ 60	+ 4
7.	5,182 =	5,000	+ 100	+ 80	+ 2
8.	614 =	0	+ 600	+ 10	+ 4
9.	4,073 =	4,000	+ 0	+ 70	+ 3
10.	9,530 =	9,000	+ 500	+ 30	+ 0

Comparing the Values of Numerals

The arrow points to the smaller number and opens wide to the larger number. 64 > 62 means that 64 is **greater than** 62.

=	>	<
means equal to	means greater than	means less than

Study the example above. Then, use >, <, or = to compare each set of numerals.

1. 72 $>$ 27

2. 61 $>$ 60

3. 34 $<$ 43

4. 27 $=$ 27

5. 23 $<$ 32

6. 98 $>$ 96

7. 82 $<$ 83

8. 56 $<$ 65

9. 18 $=$ 18

10. 49 $<$ 50

Rounding to the Nearest Hundred

When **rounding** to the nearest hundred, use these rules:

1. Look at the tens place.
2. If the number in the tens place is 0, 1, 2, 3, or 4, round down.
3. If the number in the tens place is 5, 6, 7, 8, or 9, round up.

You have discovered a hidden treasure! Study the rules above for rounding. Then, estimate the value in each treasure chest. Round these amounts to the nearest hundred. The first one is done for you.

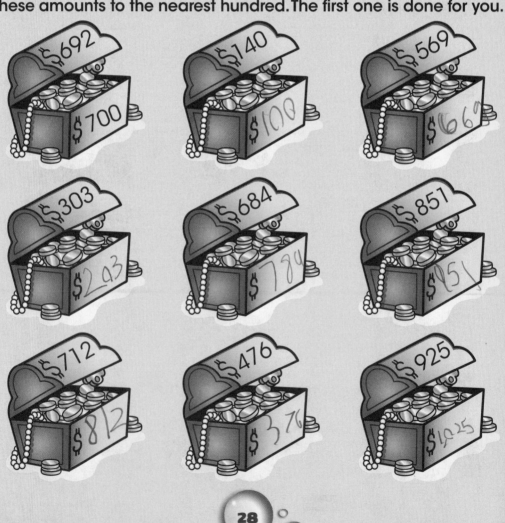

$692 → $700

$140 → $100

$569 → $66?

$303 → $293

$684 → $789

$851 → $851

$712 → $812

$476 → $376

$925 → $1,025

Skip Counting

Skip counting means following a given pattern as you count. You are probably used to counting by twos, fives, and tens. Use the number line to "skip" the given number of times.

Count by fives.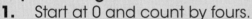

Study the example above. Then, color the number boxes to show skip counting.

1. Start at 0 and count by fours.

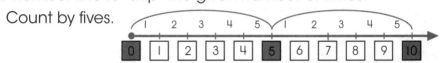

2. Start at 0 and count by sixes.

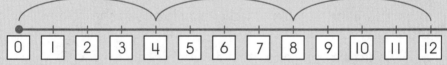

3. Start at 33 and count by threes.

4. Start at 62 and count by twos.

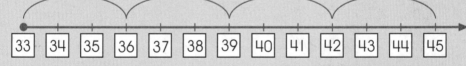

5. Start at 84 and count by fours.

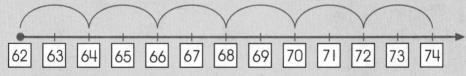

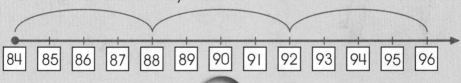

Animal Poem

Read the poem below.

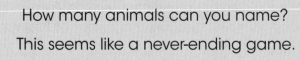

How many animals can you name?
This seems like a never-ending game.

There are little ants so very small.
There are spotted giraffes so very tall.

There are mammals and insects to name a few.
There are reptiles and amphibians in the zoo.

There are animals that fly and some that walk.
There are cows in a herd and birds in a flock.

There are animals on land and at sea.
There are animals in the ground and some in trees.

There are animals that are wild and some that are tame.
There are too many animals for us to ever name!

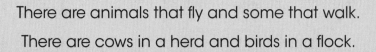

Animal Poem

After reading "Animal Poem," answer the following questions.

1. What is the main idea of the poem?
   - A. There are too many animals to name.
   - B. Animals make great pets.
   - C. Some animals are wild, and some are tame.

2. Three animals that are mentioned by name in the poem are
   - A. giraffes, ants, and cows.
   - B. sea animals, cows, and ants.
   - C. sea turtles, crows, and ants.

3. Draw a line between antonyms.

land	tame
ground	sky
wild	tall
few	sea
small	many

4. Find five plural nouns in the poem. Write them on the lines.

   _____

   _____

   _____

   _____

   _____

   _____

Cross out the animal that does not belong in each group.

5. hawk   owl
   whale   robin

6. horse   cow
   sheep   giraffe

7. squirrel   monkey
   dog   koala

8. snake   ant
   cricket   grasshopper

9. tiger   lion
   rabbit   leopard

31

The Dead Sea

The main idea of a passage tells what the passage is about. It does not tell one part or fact from the passage. It is an overview of the entire passage or paragraph. Titles often tell you something about the main idea.

Which title best describes the passage below?

Tall Buildings in the U.S.   *The Willis Tower*

The Willis Tower is the tallest building in the United States. It is even taller than the Empire State Building in New York City. The Willis Tower has 110 stories and is 1,707 feet tall (including its antenna towers on top). When the sky is clear, visitors on top of the building can see into four states!

The best title is *The Willis Tower* because the whole passage is about the Willis Tower. The Empire State Building is mentioned, but only to compare it with the Willis Tower.

Each title below describes the main idea for a different passage on page 33. Write each title at the top of its matching passage. Remember to ask yourself, "Does this title tell about the whole passage?"

The Water Cycle of the Dead Sea
What Is the Dead Sea?
The Uses of the Dead Sea
The Salty Waters of the Dead Sea

The Dead Sea

Use the titles on page 32 to tell the main idea of each passage below.

_____ _____	_____ _____
1. The Dead Sea is a saltwater lake in Asia, located between Jordan and Israel. The northern part of the lake is the deepest, measuring about 2,622 feet below sea level. At the southern end of the Dead Sea, a shallow area is partly cut off by a peninsula.	**2.** The Dead Sea is nearly nine times saltier than the ocean! The salt is so thick that very little plant or animal life can survive in its waters. The sea is believed to have gotten its name for this reason. If a person tries to swim in the Dead Sea, he will float on top!
_____ _____	_____ _____
3. The Dead Sea is useful for many reasons. Its salt is mined easily and inexpensively. Its waters are used for beauty and health reasons. Many queens, kings, and famous people have been to the sea for health or beauty reasons. Thousands of people still visit the sea in hopes of curing skin and bone problems.	**4.** The Dead Sea gets water from a river to the north called the Jordan River, which empties into the sea. Other smaller streams also feed water into the Dead Sea, mostly from the east. There are no rivers that lead out of the sea, so the water stays there until it evaporates. Because the Dead Sea is located in the desert, evaporation is fast!

Two-Digit Addition with Regrouping

1. Add the ones column. Eight plus 4 equals 12. **Regroup** to the tens column.	2. Add the tens column. Six plus 2 plus 1 equals 9.
$\begin{array}{r} 1 \\ 6\,8 \\ +\,2\,4 \\ \hline 2 \end{array}$	$\begin{array}{r} 1 \\ 6\,8 \\ +\,2\,4 \\ \hline 9\,2 \end{array}$

Study the example above. Then, solve each problem.

1.
27 + 24 = 61
39 + 53 = 92
46 + 35 = 81
57 + 29 = 86
49 + 15

2.
75 + 19 = 94
93 + 37 = 130
58 + 34 = 92
64 + 28 = 92
86 + 17 = 103

3.
66 + 26 = 92
79 + 32 = 111
43 + 27 = 70
56 + 58 = 114
98 + 32 = 130

4.
64 + 17 = 81
57 + 26 = 83
34 + 49 = 83
25 + 36 = 61
18 + 28 = 46

5.
43 + 27 = 70
26 + 36 = 62
27 + 69 = 96
53 + 37 = 90
33 + 48 = 81

Three-Digit Addition

1. Add the ones column. Two plus 4 equals 6.	2. Add the tens column. Six plus 3 equals 9.	3. Add the hundreds column. Four plus 1 equals 5.
$\begin{array}{r} 46\mathbf{2} \\ +13\mathbf{4} \\ \hline \mathbf{6} \end{array}$	$\begin{array}{r} 4\mathbf{6}2 \\ +1\mathbf{3}4 \\ \hline \mathbf{9}6 \end{array}$	$\begin{array}{r} \mathbf{4}62 \\ +\mathbf{1}34 \\ \hline \mathbf{5}96 \end{array}$

Study the example above. Then, solve each problem.

1.

$\begin{array}{r} 182 \\ +703 \\ \hline 885 \end{array}$
$\begin{array}{r} 231 \\ +547 \\ \hline 778 \end{array}$
$\begin{array}{r} 825 \\ +163 \\ \hline 988 \end{array}$
$\begin{array}{r} 436 \\ +562 \\ \hline 998 \end{array}$
$\begin{array}{r} 325 \\ +202 \\ \hline 527 \end{array}$

2.

$\begin{array}{r} 274 \\ +320 \\ \hline 594 \end{array}$
$\begin{array}{r} 641 \\ +345 \\ \hline 986 \end{array}$
$\begin{array}{r} 908 \\ +61 \\ \hline 968 \end{array}$
$\begin{array}{r} 365 \\ +424 \\ \hline 789 \end{array}$
$\begin{array}{r} 207 \\ +712 \\ \hline 919 \end{array}$

3.

$\begin{array}{r} 352 \\ +436 \\ \hline 788 \end{array}$
$\begin{array}{r} 475 \\ +510 \\ \hline 985 \end{array}$
$\begin{array}{r} 724 \\ +143 \\ \hline 867 \end{array}$
$\begin{array}{r} 650 \\ +227 \\ \hline 877 \end{array}$
$\begin{array}{r} 298 \\ +500 \\ \hline 798 \end{array}$

4.

$\begin{array}{r} 525 \\ +261 \\ \hline 786 \end{array}$
$\begin{array}{r} 631 \\ +155 \\ \hline 786 \end{array}$
$\begin{array}{r} 447 \\ +432 \\ \hline 879 \end{array}$
$\begin{array}{r} 319 \\ +450 \\ \hline 769 \end{array}$
$\begin{array}{r} 752 \\ +136 \\ \hline 888 \end{array}$

5.

$\begin{array}{r} 933 \\ +52 \\ \hline 985 \end{array}$
$\begin{array}{r} 547 \\ +131 \\ \hline 678 \end{array}$
$\begin{array}{r} 830 \\ +69 \\ \hline 899 \end{array}$
$\begin{array}{r} 626 \\ +331 \\ \hline 957 \end{array}$
$\begin{array}{r} 487 \\ +411 \\ \hline 898 \end{array}$

Four-Digit Addition

Study the examples on page 35. Then, solve each problem.

1.
```
  11          11            1          1 1       1 1
  3,261       4,639       7,216       5,952      1,794
+ 5,239     + 2,073     + 2,593     + 3,128    + 2,607
  8,500       8,712       9,809       9,080      4,411
```

2.
```
  1 1         1 1           1           1          1
  2,773       9,076       6,415       4,701      8,213
+ 3,535     + 3,970     + 1,765     + 6,354    + 1,529
  6,308      13,146       8,180      11,055      9,742
```

3.
```
  1  1         1           1   1          1          1
  3,257       9,935       1,224       6,597      4,165
+ 4,809     + 1,260     + 8,967     + 3,212    + 7,042
  8,066      11,195      10,191       9,809     11,207
```

4.
```
   11          11           1  1         1
  7,309       3,295       5,716       6,907      8,813
+ 4,597     + 4,305     + 1,708     + 4,132    + 2,076
 11,906       7,600       7,424      11,039     10,889
```

5.
```
  1 1          1           1  11          1          1
  1,943       2,967       3,846       6,381      5,490
+ 3,065     + 7,120     + 2,195     + 5,436    + 6,327
  5,008      10,087       6,041      11,817     11,817
```

Adding Money

To find the sum of several numbers, use the same steps as before:
1. Add the ones column. Regroup if necessary.
2. Add the tens column. Regroup if necessary.
3. Add the hundreds column. Regroup if necessary.
4. Add the thousands column.

When adding money, be sure to include the **decimal point** and the **dollar sign** in your answer.

Which is the richest kingdom? Study the examples on pages 34 and 35. Then, solve each problem. Be sure to include the money symbols. Color the answers on the castles. The first castle to be completely shaded is in the richest kingdom!

1.
$1.36
2.07
+ 3.64
$7.07

$6.77
3.52
+ 1.08
$11.37

$2.09
0.33
+ 9.81
$12.27

2.
$3.07
4.12
+ 6.31
$13.50

$0.94
8.41
+ 7.18
$15.53

$1.46
3.72
+ 5.40
$10.58

3.
$3.73
3.19
+ 6.42
$13.34

$7.17
8.01
+ 2.90
$18.08

$4.36
5.56
+ 9.12
$18.04

4.
$5.71
0.09
+ 0.83
$6.63

$1.80
9.84
+ 1.06
$12.70

Castle values: $13.50, $6.63, $10.58, $12.70, $13.34, $7.07

$16.53, $12.38, $11.37, $18.08, $12.23, $19.04

37

What Happens?

Drawing conclusions means using the information in a story to make a logical guess.

Read each passage. Circle the letter for each sentence that is a reasonable conclusion. Some passages have more than one answer.

1. Minnie was glad to be home after two hours of ballet practice. She could hear crickets in the woods outside her window as she turned to chapter four in her book. As she finished the chapter, she pulled the covers back to turn off the light. She burst into laughter when she looked down and realized what she was wearing.

   A. Minnie forgot to take off her dance tutu.
   B. Minnie had already washed her face.
   C. Minnie stayed up past her bedtime.
   D. Minnie had read part of the book before.

2. Murphy's mom quickly pulled everything out of the dryer. Then, she lifted the lid of the washer, looked inside, and shook her head. She looked around the kitchen and family room, then she rushed upstairs. "I cannot find them," she called to Murphy. "The last time I saw them was after your game on Saturday. We have to find them before 4:00!"

   A. Murphy's mom has friends coming over at 4:00.
   B. Murphy's mom is looking for Murphy's football pants.
   C. Murphy has a game today at 4:00.
   D. Murphy's mom lost her purse.

3. Tia walked slowly to the end of the board and looked down at the water. She wanted to jump, but her feet would not cooperate. She turned and walked back, then climbed down the ladder. "Next time," she told herself.

   A. Tia's friends can jump off the diving board.
   B. Tia is swimming.
   C. Tia wants to jump.
   D. Tia is nervous.

Mammals or Birds?

> When you read to find information, similarities and differences can help you learn more.

Bats are amazing animals. They have ears and noses like other mammals, but they have wings like birds. Or do they? Scientists have found that a bat's wing bones are like human hands. A bat has a thumb and four fingers that form each wing. The wings are not covered in feathers, but with a thick skin. Baby bats are born alive and drink milk from their mothers, like all mammals. So, are they mammals or birds?

To help you decide whether bats are mammals or birds, make a list of similarities and differences below.

Bats and Mammals	**Bats and Birds**
Alike: _____	Alike: _____
_____	_____
_____	_____
_____	_____
Different: _____	Different: _____
_____	_____
_____	_____
_____	_____

What have you concluded? Is a bat a bird or mammal? Why?

_____

_____

_____

Who's Prince Charming?

Read the story below. Then, answer the questions on page 41.

With the help of her fairy godmother, Cinderella makes it to the ball. However, when she arrives she is greeted by five handsome gentlemen. At first, Cinderella becomes upset. She is afraid she will never find the right prince! Then, she remembers the handbook her fairy godmother gave her. She pulls it from her purse and begins reading. Use the clues in the handbook to help Cinderella find her Prince Charming.

How to Tell a Real Prince from a Fake

1. A real prince always wears a crown.

2. A real prince always wears a ring on his right hand.

3. A real prince never wears a wristwatch.

4. A real prince never wears sneakers.

5. A real prince always wears shirts with exactly seven buttons.

Who's Prince Charming?

After reading "Who's Charming?," answer the following questions.

1. Circle the real Prince Charming on page 40.

2. Write a *T* next to the sentences that are true. Write an *F* next to the sentences that are false.

____ The fairy godmother helped Cinderella get to the ball.

____ The fairy godmother gave Cinderella a handbook.

____ The real prince wears a wristwatch.

____ The real prince wears sneakers.

____ The real prince wears a ring on his right hand and a crown.

Draw a line between the two words that make up each compound word.

3. gentlemen

4. horseshoe

5. handbook

6. godmother

7. wristwatch

8. What else do you think might have been in the handbook the fairy godmother gave to Cinderella?

_____

_____

_____

Underline the verb, circle the subject, and mark an X on the object in each sentence.

9. The prince's shirt has exactly seven buttons.

10. The prince is wearing a crown.

11. Cinderella read the book.

Write an antonym of each bold word.

12. The princes were **handsome**.

_____

13. Cinderella becomes **upset**.

_____

14. She fears she will never **find** her prince.

_____

15. Do you think Cinderella will **remember** her handbook?

_____

Week 4

Two-Digit Subtraction with Regrouping

1. Subtract the ones column. You cannot subtract 7 from 2, so regroup.

$$\begin{array}{r} 4\,\mathbf{2} \\ -\ 2\,\mathbf{7} \\ \hline \end{array}$$

2. To regroup, take 1 ten from the 4 tens, leaving 3 tens. Add the ten to the ones to make 12 ones. Subtract. Twelve minus 7 equals 5.

$$\begin{array}{r} {}^3\cancel{4}\,{}^1 2 \\ -\ 2\,7 \\ \hline 5 \end{array}$$

3. Subtract the tens column. Three tens minus 2 tens equals 1 ten.

$$\begin{array}{r} {}^3\cancel{4}\,{}^1 2 \\ -\ 2\,7 \\ \hline 1\,5 \end{array}$$

Study the example above. Then, solve each problem.

1.
36 − 17 = 19
98 − 19 = 79
28 − 9 = 19
41 − 15 = 26
33 − 17

2.
72 − 53 = 19
85 − 27 = 69
43 − 29 = 24
96 − 37 = 59
64 − 36

3.
47 − 19 = 28
94 − 26 = 68
75 − 39 = 36
61 − 22 = 39
33 − 19 = 14

4.
71 − 46 = 25
86 − 47 = 39
94 − 35 = 09
65 − 27 = 38
92 − 44 = 48

5.
78 − 38 = 38
64 − 35 = 29
76 − 27 = 49
52 − 44 = 08
83 − 25 = 58

42

Three Digit Subtraction

1. Subtract the ones column.	2. Subtract the tens column.	3. Subtract the hundreds column.
5 6 **4** − 1 3 **2** **2**	5 **6** 4 − 1 **3** 2 **3** 2	**5** 6 4 − **1** 3 2 **4** 3 2

Study the example above. Then, solve each problem.

1.
| 684
− 253
431 | 634
− 421
213 | 835
− 610
225 | 738
− 502
236 | 325
− 102
223 |

2.
| 874
− 321
553 | 647
− 325
322 | 958
− 146
812 | 363
− 242
121 | 567
− 362
205 |

3.
| 283
− 220
063 | 488
− 351
137 | 695
− 233
462 | 719
− 305
414 | 894
− 752
142 |

4.
| 975
− 342
633 | 767
− 425
342 | 836
− 132
704 | 547
− 235
312 | 658
− 510
148 |

5.
| 393
− 173
220 | 649
− 235
414 | 786
− 526
260 | 999
− 683
316 | 887
− 346
541 |

Two-Digit Mixed Practice

Study the examples on pages 34 and 42. Then, solve each problem.

1.

$$\begin{array}{r} 87 \\ -\ 29 \\ \hline 58 \end{array}$$

$$\begin{array}{r} 29 \\ +\ 37 \\ \hline 66 \end{array}$$

$$\begin{array}{r} 51 \\ -\ 23 \\ \hline 28 \end{array}$$

$$\begin{array}{r} 26 \\ +\ 45 \\ \hline 61 \end{array}$$

$$\begin{array}{r} 35 \\ +\ 57 \\ \hline 99 \end{array}$$

2.

$$\begin{array}{r} 91 \\ -\ 67 \\ \hline 24 \end{array}$$

$$\begin{array}{r} 86 \\ -\ 27 \\ \hline 59 \end{array}$$

$$\begin{array}{r} 71 \\ -\ 52 \\ \hline 19 \end{array}$$

$$\begin{array}{r} 62 \\ +\ 19 \\ \hline 81 \end{array}$$

$$\begin{array}{r} 53 \\ -\ 21 \\ \hline 32 \end{array}$$

3.

$$\begin{array}{r} 47 \\ +\ 13 \\ \hline 60 \end{array}$$

$$\begin{array}{r} 84 \\ +\ 58 \\ \hline 142 \end{array}$$

$$\begin{array}{r} 31 \\ -\ 19 \\ \hline 12 \end{array}$$

$$\begin{array}{r} 93 \\ -\ 36 \\ \hline 57 \end{array}$$

$$\begin{array}{r} 44 \\ +\ 48 \\ \hline 92 \end{array}$$

4.

$$\begin{array}{r} 72 \\ -\ 39 \\ \hline 33 \end{array}$$

$$\begin{array}{r} 28 \\ +\ 57 \\ \hline 85 \end{array}$$

$$\begin{array}{r} 49 \\ -\ 31 \\ \hline 18 \end{array}$$

$$\begin{array}{r} 62 \\ +\ 25 \\ \hline 87 \end{array}$$

$$\begin{array}{r} 98 \\ -\ 37 \\ \hline 61 \end{array}$$

5.

$$\begin{array}{r} 88 \\ -\ 49 \\ \hline 39 \end{array}$$

$$\begin{array}{r} 29 \\ +\ 18 \\ \hline 47 \end{array}$$

$$\begin{array}{r} 77 \\ -\ 58 \\ \hline 19 \end{array}$$

$$\begin{array}{r} 66 \\ +\ 26 \\ \hline 92 \end{array}$$

$$\begin{array}{r} 11 \\ +\ 78 \\ \hline 89 \end{array}$$

Out of This World!

Start from the center numeral and work out to solve each problem.

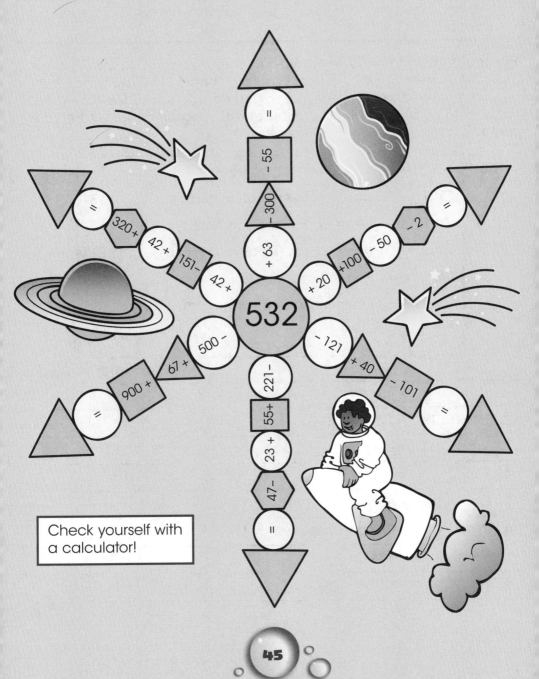

Starting from center **532**:

Up: − 300, − 55, =

Upper-left: + 42, 151 −, 42 +, 320 +, =

Upper-right: + 63, + 20, + 100, − 50, − 2, =

Left: 500 −, 67 +, 900 +, =

Right: − 121, + 40, − 101, =

Down: 221 −, 55 +, 23 +, 47 −, =

Check yourself with a calculator!

Animals

Most chapter books and longer informational books have table of contents pages after the title pages. A table of contents page helps the reader find parts of a book more quickly.

Your teacher asks you to write a report about animals. In the report, you must answer all of the questions listed below. It would take a very long time to read the entire book, so you decide to use the table of contents to help you. Write the chapter and page number where you would look to answer each question.

	Chapter	Page
1. How long do lions live?	2	13
2. How fast do sailfish swim?	4	35
3. What do snakes eat?	2	13
4. How long does it take for robin eggs to hatch?	6	57
5. Do spiders bite?	5	49
6. Where do poison dart frogs live?	3	21
7. What do beavers eat?	1	3
8. How long do turtles live?	2	13

What's In Here?

An **index** is found in the back of many informational books. It contains the main subjects covered in the book and their page numbers. An index lists the main headings for each subject area in alphabetical order. Under each main heading, more specific details might be listed in alphabetical order.

Index	
Horses	55, 57–59
Houses	
Cave	34, 41–50
Modern	14, 18, 21
American Indians	67
Humans	
Adults	115–121, 127
Babies	89, 94–108
Children	109–114
Hunting	51, 56
Hurricanes	12, 17

Use the index to find and circle the correct answers.

1. Which page will not help you learn about babies?
   A. page 89   **B.** page 92   **C.** page 97

2. Which page will help you learn about hunting?
   A. page 12   **B.** page 56   **C.** page 115

3. Which type of house is not found in the book?
   A. cave   **B.** modern   **C.** shingle

4. Which page will not help you learn about houses?
   A. page 76   **B.** page 45   **C.** page 18

5. What will you learn about on page 111?
   A. adults   **B.** children   **C.** babies

Betsy Ross

Read the passage below.

   Betsy Ross was an American hero. She did not fight in wars. She did not become president. She was simply a seamstress. But, her contribution is still remembered today. Betsy Ross made the first United States flag.

   In her journal, Betsy Ross wrote about meeting with George Washington in May of 1776. Betsy attended the same church as George Washington. He was a general at the time and asked Betsy to create a flag for the new country that would soon earn its independence. In July of 1776, the Declaration of Independence declared that the United States was independent from Britain. On June 14, 1777, Congress decided that the flag Betsy Ross made would be the flag of the United States. The flag was to represent the unity of the 13 colonies as one country. The new flag was first flown over Fort Stanwix, New York, on August 3, 1777.

   Today, the U.S. flag has 50 stars, representing the country's 50 states. The 13 stripes represent the 13 original colonies. Americans continue to honor the flag and the freedom it represents by saying the Pledge of Allegiance and singing "The Star-Spangled Banner." The U.S. government set aside June 14th as Flag Day to honor the flag.

Betsy Ross

After reading "Betsy Ross," answer the following questions.

1. What is Betsy Ross best remembered for?
   - A. fighting in a war
   - B. marrying the president
   - C. making the first flag

2. How did Betsy Ross know George Washington?
   - A. He was the president.
   - B. He was her brother.
   - C. They went to the same church.

3. Circle the letter of the sentence that is true.
   - A. The stars on the flag represent the 50 states, and the stripes represent the 13 colonies.
   - B. The stars on the flag represent the 50 states, and the stripes represent the number of battles won to gain independence.
   - C. The stars on the flag represent the 50 heroes of the war, and the stripes represent the 13 colonies.

4. The prefix *uni-* means "one." Write two other words that have the prefix *uni-*.

   _____

   _____

Write each syllable of the words below in the blanks. Use a dictionary to help.

5. contribution _____ _____ _____ _____

6. attended _____ _____ _____

7. representing _____ _____ _____ _____

8. allegiance _____ _____ _____

Read the index below. Then, answer the questions.

Colonies 5, 7–9, 22

Flags 10, 15, 18–20

Heroes 6, 28–30

Holidays 19, 25

9. On what pages could you find the names of the 13 colonies? _____

10. What pages might have information about the life of Paul Revere? _____

11. On what pages could you find information on Independence Day?

    _____

49

Introduction to Multiplication

To **multiply** means to use repeated addition. The answer to a multiplication problem is called the **product**. The numbers being multiplied are called **factors**. To more easily understand, imagine making equal groups. Then, add all of the groups together. Multiplication looks like this:

$$4 + 4 + 4$$
3 groups of 4
$$3 \times 4 \leftarrow \text{factors}$$
$$12 \leftarrow \text{product}$$

Study the example above. Then, write an addition and multiplication problem for each picture. Find the sum and the product.

1.
×××××
×××××
×××××

$5 + 5 + 5 = 15$
$5 \times 3 = 15$

2.
☆☆☆
☆☆☆

$2 + 3 = 6$
$3 \times 2 = 6$

3.

$2 + 2 + 2 + 2 = 8$
$4 \times 2 = 8$

4.

$4 + 4 = 8$
$4 \times 2 = 8$

5.
× × ×
× × ×
× × ×

$3 + 3 + 3 = 9$
$3 \times 3 = 9$

6.
☆☆☆☆
☆☆☆☆
☆☆☆☆

$4 + 4 + 4 = 12$
$4 \times 3 = 12$

7.

$2 + 2 + 2 = 6$
$2 \times 3 = 6$

8.

$5 + 5 = 10$
$5 \times 2 = 10$

Finding the Facts

Study the example on page 50. Then, find the product for each pair of factors below. Use the code to find the letters. Write the letters on the lines to answer the two riddles.

A	B	C	D	E	F	G	H	I	J	K	L	M	N	O	P	Q	R	S	T	U	V	W	X	Y	Z
64	4	42	7	24	16	0	18	40	11	19	49	59	25	13	12	21	56	8	54	32	28	45	60	9	14

What can you hold in your left hand but not in your right hand?

Y   O   U   R
3 x 3   6 x 2   8 x 4   7 x 8

R   I   G   H   T
8 x 7   5 x 8   1 x 0   6 x 3   6 x 9

E   L   B   O   W !
8 x 3   7 x 7   2 x 2   3 x 4   9 x 5

Why is it so easy to weigh fish?

B   E   C   A   U   S   E
4 x 1   6 x 4   6 x 7   8 x 8   4 x 8   2 x 4   3 x 8

F   I   S   H   H   A   V   E
4 x 4   8 x 5   1 x 8   9 x 2   3 x 6   8 x 8   7 x 4   4 x 6

T   H   E   I   R   O   W   N
9 x 6   2 x 9   8 x 3   5 x 8   7 x 8   3 x 4   9 x 5   5 x 5

S   C   A   L   E   S !
4 x 2   7 x 6   8 x 8   7 x 7   6 x 4   8 x 1

8+8=16
8+8=24
12+8=32
3×2+8=40
4+8=48
8+8=56
9×8=64
64+8=72

51

Two-Digit Multiplication

First, multiply the ones. Then, multiply the tens. Add.

$$\begin{array}{r} 1\,\mathbf{2} \\ \times \quad \mathbf{3} \\ \hline \mathbf{6} \end{array}$$
+
$$\begin{array}{r} 1\,2 \\ \times \quad \mathbf{3} \\ \hline \mathbf{3\,0} \end{array} = 36$$

Shortcut:

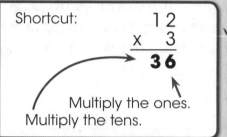

$$\begin{array}{r} 1\,2 \\ \times \quad 3 \\ \hline \mathbf{3\,6} \end{array}$$

Multiply the ones.
Multiply the tens.

Study the example above. Then, solve each problem.

1.
$$\begin{array}{r} 12 \\ \times\ 4 \\ \hline 48 \end{array}$$
$$\begin{array}{r} 11 \\ \times\ 2 \\ \hline 22 \end{array}$$
$$\begin{array}{r} 13 \\ \times\ 2 \\ \hline 26 \end{array}$$
$$\begin{array}{r} 13 \\ \times\ 3 \\ \hline \end{array}$$

2.
$$\begin{array}{r} 11 \\ \times\ 3 \\ \hline 33 \end{array}$$
$$\begin{array}{r} 14 \\ \times\ 2 \\ \hline 28 \end{array}$$
$$\begin{array}{r} 12 \\ \times\ 3 \\ \hline 36 \end{array}$$
$$\begin{array}{r} 11 \\ \times\ 4 \\ \hline \end{array}$$

3.
$$\begin{array}{r} 13 \\ \times\ 1 \\ \hline 13 \end{array}$$
$$\begin{array}{r} 11 \\ \times\ 6 \\ \hline 66 \end{array}$$
$$\begin{array}{r} 22 \\ \times\ 3 \\ \hline 66 \end{array}$$
$$\begin{array}{r} 32 \\ \times\ 2 \\ \hline \end{array}$$

4.
$$\begin{array}{r} 42 \\ \times\ 2 \\ \hline 84 \end{array}$$
$$\begin{array}{r} 24 \\ \times\ 2 \\ \hline 48 \end{array}$$
$$\begin{array}{r} 22 \\ \times\ 2 \\ \hline 44 \end{array}$$
$$\begin{array}{r} 21 \\ \times\ 3 \\ \hline \end{array}$$

5.
$$\begin{array}{r} 33 \\ \times\ 3 \\ \hline 99 \end{array}$$
$$\begin{array}{r} 32 \\ \times\ 3 \\ \hline 96 \end{array}$$
$$\begin{array}{r} 31 \\ \times\ 3 \\ \hline 93 \end{array}$$
$$\begin{array}{r} 31 \\ \times\ 2 \\ \hline \end{array}$$

Two-Digit Multiplication with Regrouping

First, multiply the ones. Then, multiply the tens. Add.

$$\begin{array}{r}1\!\!\!3\\ \times\ 6\\ \hline 18\end{array} + \begin{array}{r}13\\ \times\ 6\\ \hline 60\end{array} = 78$$

Shortcut:
Multiply the ones.
Regroup to the tens.

$$\begin{array}{r}1\\ 13\\ \times\ 6\\ \hline 78\end{array}$$

Multiply the tens.
6 x 10 = 60
Add the extra ten.
60 + 10 = 70

Study the example above. Then, solve each problem.

1.
15 × 6 = 90
14 × 5 = 70
13 × 7 = 91
24 × 3 = 72
22 × 5 = 110

2.
12 × 7 = 84
25 × 4 = 100
32 × 6 = 192
23 × 7 = 161
14 × 8 = 112

3.
26 × 3 = 78
52 × 6 = 132
44 × 5 = 220
34 × 6 = 204
13 × 9 = 117

4.
84 × 3 = 252
45 × 6 = 270
32 × 9 = 288
16 × 7 = 112
28 × 2 = 56

5.
35 × 6 = 210
18 × 7 = 126
22 × 7 = 154
34 × 5 = 170
47 × 3 = 141

53

Animal World

> **Sequence** is the order in which a set of events happen. Sequencing provides order and helps you make sense of what you read.

A schedule helps you see the order of events more clearly. Use the schedule below to answer the questions.

Our Day at Animal World	
10:45–11:15	The Reptile Review
11:20–11:45	Elsie the Elephant Show
11:45–12:15	Lunch at the Penguin Palace
12:30–1:00	Sea Lion Show
1:10–1:45	Birds of Prey
2:00–4:45	The Monkey Movie
5:00–6:00	Dinner at the Coyote Café
6:10–6:25	Wildcat Wackiness
6:30–7:00	Penguins on Parade

1. Which show is after the Sea Lion Show? _Lunch at the penguin place_

2. Is lunch before or after the Elephant Show? _After_

3. Which shows are after dinner?

   Penguins on parade and _Wildcat Wackiness_

4. Which show is before the Elephant Show? _The reptile Review_

5. What will be happening at 3:00? _Lunch_

6. Where will lunch be? _rateri pku_

Key Words

Key words are often used to provide the reader clues about the sequence of a story's events. Words like *first, then, next,* and *last* are examples of key words.

Use the key words to decide which sentence in each pair comes first. Label the sentences 1 and 2. Then, underline the key words that helped you decide.

1. ____ Before, I walked to school.
   ____ Now, I take the bus to school.

2. ____ Football practice starts soon.
   ____ School starts immediately.

3. ____ First, you need to clean your room.
   ____ Next, you need to fold your clothes.

4. ____ She did her math homework earlier.
   ____ She is finally doing her spelling homework.

5. ____ We need to get to swim lessons right away.
   ____ We need to get to piano lessons eventually.

6. ____ My parents said that we will get a puppy someday.
   ____ My parents said that we will get a fish soon.

7. ____ My mom says that I will learn to like asparagus eventually.
   ____ My mom says that I will never learn to like broccoli.

8. ____ My teacher will send my test scores home later this week.
   ____ My teacher will send my report card home today.

Sara and Katie

Read each pair of sentences. If they tell how Sara's life is the same as Katie's, circle the word same. If they tell how Sara's life is different from Katie's, circle the word _different_.

A girl named Katie lives in a desert town not far from Sara's home. In some ways, Katie's life is like Sara's. In other ways, their lives are very different.

1. Sara is a desert tortoise. Katie is a girl.   same   different

2. Sara lives in a burrow. Katie lives in a house.   same   different

3. Sara eats in the morning. Katie does, too.   same   different

4. Sara can live for more than 60 years. Katie can, too.   same   different

5. Sara does not have wings. Katie doesn't either.   same   different

6. Sara can go for years without drinking water. Katie needs water every day.   same   different

7. Sara sleeps all winter. Katie does not.   same   different

8. Sara has four legs. Katie has two.   same   different

Extra!
Think of more ways Sara and Katie are the same.

Alike or Different?

Part of reading carefully is watching for ways that things are alike (similarities) and ways that they are different (differences).

Each of the items below are probably familiar to you. Imagine that you are comparing them for a friend who cannot see them. How are the two items in each pair alike? How are they different? Write one similarity and one difference for each pair.

1.

These items are similar because

They both are tools.

These items are different because

They don't do the same thing.

2.

These items are similar because

They both have flowers

These items are different because

One is real

3.

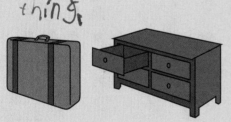

These items are similar because

They both open .

These items are different because

One you can carry .

4.

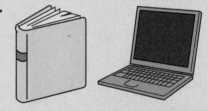

These items are similar because

They both have wo

These items are different because

One uses electricity .

Introduction to Division

To **divide** means to make equal groups or to share equally. The answer to a division problem is called the **quotient**. Division looks like this:

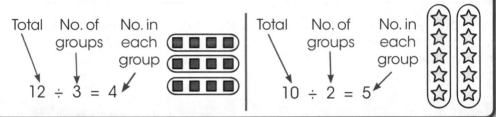

Total   No. of   No. in
         groups   each
                   group

$12 \div 3 = 4$

Total   No. of   No. in
         groups   each
                   group

$10 \div 2 = 5$

Study the examples above. Then, circle equal groups to find the quotient for each picture.

1.

☆ ☆ ☆ ☆ ☆
☆ ☆ ☆ ☆ ☆

$10 \div 5 = \boxed{2}$

2.

■ ■ ■ ■ ■
■ ■ ■ ■ ■
■ ■ ■ ■ ■

$15 \div 3 = \boxed{5}$

3.

○ ○ ○
○ ○ ○

$6 \div 3 = \boxed{2}$

4.

e e e e
e e e e

$8 \div 2 = \boxed{4}$

5.

☆ ☆ ☆
☆ ☆ ☆
☆ ☆ ☆

$9 \div 3 = \boxed{3}$

6.

■ ■ ■ ■
■ ■ ■ ■
■ ■ ■ ■

$12 \div 4 = \boxed{3}$

7.

● ● ● ● ● ●
● ● ● ● ● ●

$12 \div 6 = \boxed{2}$

8.

e e e e e e
e e e e e e
e e e e e e

$18 \div 3 = \boxed{6}$

9.

☆ ☆ ☆ ☆ ☆ ☆ ☆
☆ ☆ ☆ ☆ ☆ ☆ ☆

$14 \div 7 = \boxed{2}$

Using Division Signs

We read this problem as "12 **divided** by 3 **equals** 4." Twelve put into 3 equal groups equals 4 in each group.

$12 \div 3 = \underline{4}$

$$3\overline{)12} \quad \text{(quotient } 4\text{)}$$

Study the examples above and on page 58. Then, solve each problem. Draw a picture.

1 $9 \div 3 = \underline{3}$

  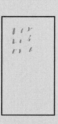

2. $8 \div 2 = \underline{4}$

 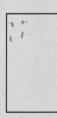

3. $6 \div 2 = \underline{3}$

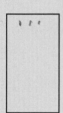 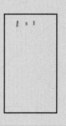

4. $16 \div 4 = \underline{\text{m}}$

 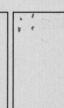

5. $12 \div 6 = \underline{2}$

6. $18 \div 3 = \underline{6}$

  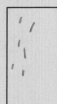

Division with Remainders

Divisor → 3)19 ← Dividend

1. Think. How many times will 3 go into 19? 3 x 6 = 18.
2. Then, subtract. What is left is the **remainder**.

$$\begin{array}{r} 6\ r1 \\ 3\overline{)19} \\ -18 \\ \hline 1 \end{array}$$

Study the example above. Then, solve each problem.

1.
2)15
-14
1

5
3)17
-15
2

4
4)19
-16
3

3r4
6)22
-18
4

2.
6
4)25
-24
1

3
5)18
-15
3

3
7)23
-21
2

5r3
8)43
-40
3

3.
7
9)70
-63
7

9
2)19
-18
1

5
4)21
-20
1

4r4
5)24
-20

4.
4
7)30
-28
2

0
6)13
-12
1

3
8)25
-24
1

6r2
5)32
-30
2

5.
4
4)17
-16
1

3
7)25
-21
4

4
9)42
-36
6

4r6
8)38
-32
6

60

Connecting Operations

Multiplication depends on equal groups. You can use multiplication basic facts to help you divide. The two are related, like families. They are called **fact families**. It looks like this:

 4 groups of 3
4 x 3 = 12

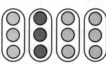 12 divided into 4 equal groups
12 ÷ 4 = 3

Study the example above. Then, use the missing factor to help you find the quotient.

1.
2 x $\boxed{4}$ = 8

8 ÷ 2 = $\boxed{4}$

2.
3 x $\boxed{3}$ = 9

9 ÷ 3 = $\boxed{3}$

3.
4 x $\boxed{4}$ = 16

16 ÷ 4 = $\boxed{4}$

4.
8 x $\boxed{5}$ = 40

40 ÷ 8 = $\boxed{5}$

5.
5 x $\boxed{5}$ = 25

25 ÷ 5 = $\boxed{5}$

6.
6 x $\boxed{3}$ = 18

18 ÷ 6 = $\boxed{3}$

7.
4 x $\boxed{3}$ = 12

12 ÷ 4 = $\boxed{3}$

8.
7 x $\boxed{6}$ = 42

42 ÷ 7 = $\boxed{6}$

9.
3 x $\boxed{5}$ = 15

15 ÷ 3 = $\boxed{5}$

10.
9 x $\boxed{9}$ = 81

81 ÷ 9 = $\boxed{9}$

11.
2 x $\boxed{5}$ = 10

10 ÷ 2 = $\boxed{5}$

12.
2 x $\boxed{2}$ = 4

4 ÷ 2 = $\boxed{2}$

13.
5 x $\boxed{4}$ = 20

20 ÷ 5 = $\boxed{4}$

14.
3 x $\boxed{2}$ = 6

6 ÷ 3 = $\boxed{2}$

15.
6 x $\boxed{6}$ = 36

36 ÷ 6 = $\boxed{6}$

What Happened?

> To make an **inference** means to make an educated guess using the information given.
>
> **Example**: *Keisha soaked up the milk with a sponge.*
> You can infer from the information that milk was probably spilled.

The sentences below imply that something has happened. Write a sentence for each telling what may have happened.

1. The boy's mom apologized to the shop owner.

Some stuff fell down.

2. The dog sat by the fire to warm himself.

Really cold day.

3. The animals scurried back into the woods.

The animals were scared

4. The boys roared with laughter.

Really funny thing.

5. Tasha swung her bat even harder the second time.

First she swung soft.

6. Marcus counted the money left in his wallet.

He paid for somthing.

The Money Plant

Read the story below.

There was a man who lived on Hills Lane. The children on the street went to visit him every day after school. The man baked cookies for them and taught them how to play games. He loved when they came to visit him.

His favorite hobby was growing plants. He had many different types of plants. The children helped him pull weeds around the plants and give them water. There was one plant that the man thought was dead. He asked the children to throw it away.

As a surprise, the children decided to nurse the plant back to health. Every day after school they crept into the backyard, where they watered and talked to the plant. The man had no idea what the children were doing.

One day, the children noticed that the plant had grown strange green leaves. They were so excited that they ran inside to tell the man about it. When the man went outside, he noticed that the strange little leaves looked just like dollar bills! Could it be that this was a money plant?

The Money Plant

The next morning, the man went to check the plant and found hundreds of dollars on the stems! He pulled the money off, and instantly more bills appeared! He was shocked. He wasn't quite sure what to do. He decided to go inside, eat breakfast, and think about how to use the money.

The man decided to give each of the children some of the money because they had cared for the plant. When the children came over that afternoon, he told them his plan. The children were very excited!

The man divided the money among the children, and they ran to their homes to share the news. The next day, the man made a special batch of cookies for his friends. He waited and waited, but they never came to visit. He thought they were out spending their money and would come to visit the next day. The next day came and went, and the children never visited. This made the man very sad.

He went outside to the backyard and pulled the money plant up by the roots. He wanted his friends to visit him to have fun, not to get money. Every morning the man made cookies, hoping to have visitors. He sat on the front porch in the afternoon, waiting to hear the sounds of the children's voices.

Several days later, the man was rocking in his chair, when he heard the children! He was thrilled. When the children came to the porch, they had cards and gifts to give him. He told them he had thrown the money plant away. They said it didn't matter and apologized for not coming to visit. The man smiled, went inside, and brought out a batch of fresh chocolate chip cookies.

The Money Plant

After reading "The Money Plant," answer the following questions.

1. What did the man enjoy most about his day?
   - **A.** baking cookies
   - **B.** visiting with the children
   - **C.** watering his plants
   - **D.** rocking on the front porch

2. What does it mean to nurse a plant back to health?
   - **A.** give the plant medicine
   - **B.** take the plant to a hospital
   - **C.** help the plant grow
   - **D.** cut the plant into pieces

3. The word *crept* in the third paragraph means
   - **A.** to sneak into.
   - **B.** to crawl under.
   - **C.** to run around.
   - **D.** to stop and look.

4. Why did the man decide to give the children the money from the plant?

   _____

   _____

5. Why did the man throw the plant away?

   _____

   _____

   _____

Telling Time

The short hand is called the **hour hand**. It tells the hour. The long hand is the **minute hand**. It tells the minutes. On the left, the clock's hour hand is on the 8. The minute hand is on the 12. It shows 8 o'clock. On the right, the clock's minute hand is on the 6. It shows 8:30. We say this as "eight-thirty."

8:00   8:30

Study the examples above. Then, write the time shown on each clock.

1.

6 : 30   11 : 00   5 : 00

2.

6 : 00   12 : 30   10 : 30

Five Minute Intervals

The minute hand takes 5 minutes to move from one number on the clock to the next. We count by fives as the minute hand moves to the next number. To read this clock, we say:

20 minutes
past 3:00

3:20

40 minutes
past 9:00

9:40

Study the examples above. Then, write each time two ways.

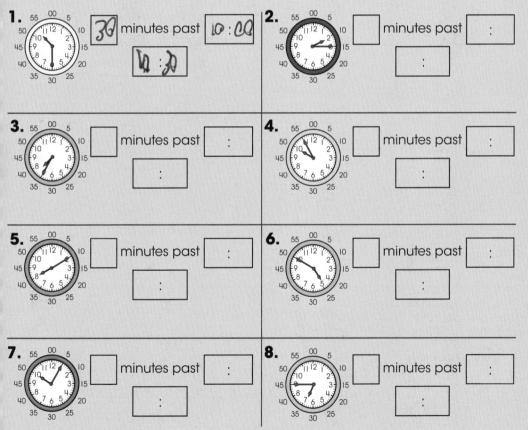

1. [30] minutes past [10 : 00]

[10 : 30]

2. [   ] minutes past [:   ]

3. [   ] minutes past [:   ]

4. [   ] minutes past [:   ]

5. [   ] minutes past [:   ]

6. [   ] minutes past [:   ]

7. [   ] minutes past [:   ]

8. [   ] minutes past [:   ]

Counting Money

We write 1 dollar as $1.00. We say $1.35 as "one dollar and thirty-five cents."

$1.35

$1.00 = 100¢ $5.00 $10.00 $20.00

Study the money values above. Then, count the money to find the total value.

1.

$1.55

2.

$2.48

3.

$3.45

4.
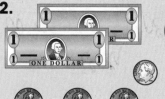

$10.85

5.

$4.17

6.

$33.22

68

Calculating Change

Sometimes when you pay for something, you get **change** back. You can figure your change using these steps:

1. Begin with the amount you paid the cashier.
2. Subtract the amount you owe from the amount you paid. Make sure to keep the **decimal points** lined up.
3. The difference is your change.

$$\begin{array}{r} {}^{4\ \ 9\ 10} \\ \$5.\cancel{00} \\ -\ 0.75 \\ \hline \$4.25 \end{array}$$

Study the example above. Then, find the amount of change that will be given to the customer.

1.	Paid Owe	$6.00 − 2.10 $3.90	**2.**	Paid Owe	$20.00 − 16.20 $3.80
3.	Paid Owe	$8.00 − 3.95 $4.05	**4.**	Paid Owe	$10.00 − 4.60 $5.40
5.	Paid Owe	$9.00 − 8.50 $0.50	**6.**	Paid Owe	$5.00 − 0.95 $4.05
7.	Paid Owe	$16.00 − 15.15 $00.85	**8.**	Paid Owe	$20.00 − 5.00 $15.00
9.	Paid Owe	$2.00 − 1.19 $0.81	**10.**	Paid Owe	$4.00 − 3.95 $0.05

The Snow Child

Read the story below.

Many years ago, there lived a woman and a man. As they grew older, they also grew sadder, for they had no children. One winter morning, the man looked out the window at the falling snow. "Let's build a snow child," he suggested to his wife. "Yes," said the woman, "a snow child just for us."

The man and the woman went outside and began to make a little girl out of snow. They made her legs, her arms, and her head. They used bits of sparkling blue ice for her eyes. When the man and woman finished, they stood back to look at what they had created. They could hardly believe their eyes. They had created a beautiful snow child. The woman kissed the snow child gently on the cheek. Suddenly, the snow child began to smile. She stretched out her arms. She stretched out her legs. She spun around and gave a little laugh. "I'm alive," she giggled with delight. Nothing could have made the couple happier.

The days passed. Soon, the winter storms turned to spring showers. The sun began to warm the earth. The signs of spring were everywhere. But, as the days became warmer, the snow child became more and more unhappy. She would not go outside. "Come, little daughter. Why do you look so sad? Go outside and play with the other children," said the woman. The snow child did as she was told.

But before the snow child could join the other children, she disappeared. There was only a white mist where the girl had stood. The mist formed into a thin cloud and rose higher and higher, until it joined the clouds in the sky. The man and the woman wept bitterly at the loss of their dear little snow child. Once again, they were sad and lonely.

After many months, the days became shorter and the nights longer. The air was crisp and cool once again. Winter was coming. One night, as the first snow began to fall, the couple sat by the window remembering their dear little snow child. Suddenly, they heard a happy laugh and a familiar voice singing,

Winter is here. I am back with the snow. Do not fear, when comes spring I go. I will return with the snow each year, for you, my parents, are oh, so dear.

The couple ran to the door. They hugged their little snow child. How happy they were to be together again! The snow child stayed with them through each winter. Then, when spring came, she disappeared until winter returned to the couple's cottage again.

The Snow Child

After reading "The Snow Child," answer the following questions.

1. Why were the man and the woman sad at the beginning of the story?
   A. because they were growing old
   B. because they had no children
   C. because the winter was too cold

2. What brought the snow child to life?
   A. a fairy godmother
   B. a snowflake
   C. the woman's kiss

The ending -er often means "more." Sometimes, it is used to compare two things. The ending -est means "most." It is used to compare more than two things. Write the correct word to complete each sentence.

3. The days are getting _____ now that summer is here.

4. That clown looks _____ than the one with the frown on his face.

5. Jessie's hair is _____ than Claudia's.

6. Ilene is three years _____ than Kevin.

Write the base word for each word below. On another sheet of paper, add -est to each word and use it in a sentence.

7. warmer _____

8. happier _____

9. shorter _____

10. older _____

11. higher _____

12. Why would the snow child disappear in the spring?
    _____
    _____
    _____

13. In the story, what are some signs of spring?
    _____
    _____
    _____

14. In the story, what are some signs of winter?
    _____
    _____
    _____

Ellen's Helpers

You can predict what could happen next by using the clues within a story.

Circle the letter of the sentence that tells what will probably happen next.

1. Ellen was excited to spend the morning at the park with her mother and her three-year-old twin brothers, Sam and Adam. Ellen offered to start packing their lunches while her mom got the boys ready to go. It was not long before Sam appeared at Ellen's feet and asked to help. Ellen explained that she was in a hurry to get to the park. Sam turned to the refrigerator and took out the grapes. The bowl was much too big for him to hold, and . . .

    A. Sam put the grapes in the lunch basket.
    B. Sam dropped the bowl.
    C. Sam ate all of the grapes.

2. Grapes went everywhere. At that moment, Adam ran into the room and slid on the grapes. Ellen grabbed the broom while her mom settled the boys in another room. As Ellen and her mom finished sweeping the floor, they heard a loud crash in the broom closet. When they went to look, they saw Sam and Adam standing in the closet with the vacuum in their hands. They wanted to help clean up the grapes, but the vacuum had fallen to the floor. The dust bag had broken open, and the boys were . . .

    A. sitting in a pile of dust.
    B. playing with their blocks.
    C. laughing at a movie.

3. Ellen and her mother quickly cleaned the boys and headed for the car. "Oh, no," said Ellen's mom. "I forgot to feed the dog." Hearing this, . . .

    A. Sam and Adam jumped into their car seats.
    B. Sam and Adam asked for a snack.
    C. Sam and Adam ran toward the big bag of dog food.

The Musicians of Bremen

Make predictions as you come to questions. Do not read ahead!

Long ago, there lived a donkey who faithfully served his master for many years. The donkey had become too old to carry sacks of grain, and his master planned to do away with him. The donkey developed a plan to run away to the town of Bremen, where he would become a musician. The donkey had not gone too far when he came upon an old hunting dog lying on the ground. The dog explained that he had become too old to hunt any longer, and that his master had plans to get rid of him.

1. What do you think will happen next?_____
_____

The donkey suggested that the dog join him in Bremen and become a musician. The dog agreed, and the two continued their journey. Farther down the road, they happened upon an old cat and an old rooster, both afraid as well. They decided to join the donkey and the dog. As night fell, the travelers became tired and hungry. They spotted a house in the woods and approached it. Peering in, they saw a table full of food and a band of robbers sitting around it. They screeched out their music as loud as they could, scaring the robbers away.

2. What do you think the four musicians will do now? _____
_____

After the animals fell asleep, the robbers came back to the house. They saw the cat's eyes reflecting light, and began to run. The dog bit their legs, the donkey kicked them, and the rooster crowed. The robbers were so scared they never returned to the house again.

3. What will the animals do now? _____
_____

Introduction to Fractions

A **fraction** tells about equal parts of a whole. The top number is the **numerator.** It tells how many parts are shaded. The bottom number is the **denominator.** It tells how many parts in all.

Parts shaded ⟶ $\dfrac{1}{6}$
Parts in all ⟶

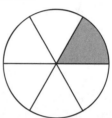

Study the example above. Then, write each fraction.

1.
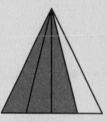
$\dfrac{1}{6}$

2.
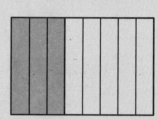
$\dfrac{3}{8}$

3.

$\dfrac{3}{4}$

4.

$\dfrac{5}{8}$

5.
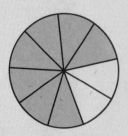
$\dfrac{7}{9}$

6.
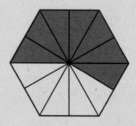
$\dfrac{7}{12}$

Equivalent Fractions

Equivalent fractions are fractions that are equal. To find equivalent fractions, multiply the numerator and the denominator of a fraction by the same number.

$$\frac{1 \times (2)}{2 \times (2)} = \frac{2}{4} \quad \frac{1 \times (3)}{2 \times (3)} = \frac{3}{6}$$

Study the example above. Then, fill in the missing numerals to show equivalent fractions.

1. $\dfrac{1}{3} = \dfrac{3}{6} = \dfrac{4}{9} = \dfrac{4}{8} = \dfrac{5}{10}$

2. $\dfrac{1}{4} = \dfrac{4}{8} = \dfrac{6}{12} = \dfrac{4}{8} = \dfrac{10}{20}$

3. $\dfrac{2}{3} = \dfrac{3}{6} = \dfrac{6}{12} = \dfrac{6}{12} = \dfrac{10}{20}$

4. $\dfrac{3}{4} = \dfrac{6}{3} = \dfrac{9}{18} = \dfrac{8}{16} = \dfrac{6}{12}$

5. $\dfrac{4}{5} = \dfrac{9}{10} \qquad \dfrac{3}{7} = \dfrac{7}{21} \qquad \dfrac{4}{7} = \dfrac{16}{22} \qquad \dfrac{3}{4} = \dfrac{21}{11}$

Using Decimals

Fractions that are tenths ($\frac{1}{10}$) or hundredths ($\frac{1}{100}$) are easy to write as decimals. Hint: When there are no whole numbers, put a zero in the ones place.

$\frac{4}{10}$ = four tenths

= 0.4

$1\frac{3}{10}$ = one and three tenths

= 1.3

$\frac{14}{100}$ = fourteen hundredths

= 0.14

$1\frac{23}{100}$ = one and twenty-three hundredths

= 1.23

Study the examples above. Then, write each fraction as a decimal number. Color the balloons with tenths blue. Color the balloons with hundredths green.

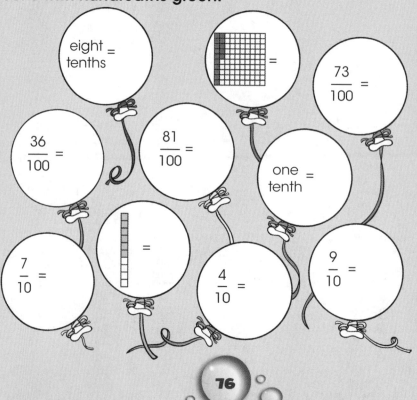

eight tenths =

=

$\frac{73}{100}$ =

$\frac{36}{100}$ =

$\frac{81}{100}$ =

one tenth =

=

$\frac{7}{10}$ =

$\frac{4}{10}$ =

$\frac{9}{10}$ =

Place Value Practice

Study the examples below. Then, write how many ones, tenths, and hundredths each decimal contains.

	ones	tenths	hundredths
0.6	0	6	0
1. 1.07	1	0	7
2. 5.60	5	6	0
3. 3.91	3	9	1
4. 16.06	16	0	6
5. 0.13	9	1	3
6. 7.93	7	9	3

	ones	tenths	hundredths
4.3	4	3	0
7. 3.01	3	0	1
8. 1.25	1	2	5
9. 4.11	4	1	1
10. 2.53	2	5	3
11. 9.1	9	1	0
12. 8.84	8	8	4

Study the examples below and on page 76. Then, solve each problem. Shade in the boxes to show your answer.

0.06 + 0.03 = ___0.09___

13. 1.46 + 0.34 = ___1.80___

14. 1.5 + 1.7 = ___3.02___

15. 2.4 + 1.8 = ___4.2___

16. 0.37 + 2.70 = ___3.07___

17. 2.55 + 1.68 = ___4.23___

Dear Donna

Read the passage below.

June 13, 2006

Dear Donna,

The other day was a bad day for my mom and me. I forgot to pick a few ears of corn from our garden for dinner, and she was upset. She even restricted me from playing outside. I can understand why she was so upset with me; I forgot to do my chores.

A few hours after she sent me to my room, I apologized to her for forgetting. I think my apology made my mom feel better, because she let me go outside to play. I was excited to use the new kite that I got for my birthday.

The sun was shining brightly, and there was just enough wind to fly my kite. After I looked at the kite flying high up in the sky, a feeling of happiness came over me. It was like magic!

The wind started to die down, so I decided to pull my kite down and go home. The minute I walked into the kitchen holding my kite, my mom smiled at me. I asked her why she was smiling. Mom told me that my red cheeks and the smile on my face made her happy!

After dinner, I went to my mom and kissed her on the cheek. She asked me why I did that. I told her that her smile made me happy. It was a good ending to a bad day. I hope to hear from you soon.

Your best friend,

Ebony

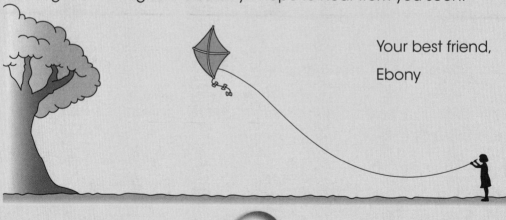

Dear Donna

After reading "Dear Donna," answer the following questions.

1. The word *restricted* means
   - **A.** vacationed.
   - **B.** confined.
   - **C.** worked.
   - **D.** played.

2. What was Ebony's punishment for not completing her chore?
   - **A.** cleaning her room
   - **B.** flying a kite
   - **C.** not playing outside
   - **D.** cleaning the dishes

3. What feeling did Ebony get when she was able to fly her kite?
   - **A.** happy
   - **B.** depressed
   - **C.** anxious
   - **D.** scared

4. What made Ebony's mother happy?
   - **A.** dinner
   - **B.** Ebony's red cheeks and smile
   - **C.** Ebony's kite
   - **D.** gardening

5. Why do you think Ebony likes to see her mother smile?

   _____

   _____

   _____

   _____

   _____

Stray Cat Hero

Read the story below.

My mom always takes in stray animals. The one I remember best was a mangy kitten.

One day, a dirty, hungry little kitten wandered onto our porch. Mom took pity on the kitten. She brought it in the house, gave it a bath, and fed it. She took special care of this kitten.

One night, we were all sound asleep. At about two in the morning, I heard loud meowing. Mom's stray kitten jumped next to my face and began to lick me. I pushed the cat away, rolled over, and went back to sleep. The persistent cat wouldn't take no for an answer. He went to my dad. My dad pushed the cat over to my mom's side of the bed. Although my mom is a very heavy sleeper, the cat continued to meow and lick her face. Finally, my mom awoke. At first, she was annoyed. But, then she realized what the cat wanted. Mom smelled gas. She immediately woke Dad. They turned the gas off and opened all of the windows. We had a gas leak that no one noticed except our stray cat. Mom's stray cat had saved us. That's how the little stray kitten became our family pet, and that's how Hero got his name!

Stray Cat Hero

After reading "Stray Cat Hero," answer the following questions.

1. Number the sentences in the order that they happened in the story.

   ____ Mom took care of a stray cat.

   ____ We named the stray cat Hero.

   ____ The cat tried to wake Dad.

   ____ The cat woke Mom.

   ____ Mom smelled gas.

   ____ Mom and Dad turned off the gas.

Cause is why something happens. Effect is the event that happens. Circle the correct answer below.

2. Because Hero woke Mom,

   A. she got scratched.

   B. she smelled the gas.

   C. the family awoke.

3. They opened all of the windows

   A. to let Hero outside.

   B. because they were hot.

   C. because there was a gas smell.

4. Mom gave the kitten a bath

   A. because no one else would.

   B. because it asked her to.

   C. because it was dirty and she felt pity for it.

Draw a line between the present tense and past tense of each word.

5. take   brought

6. become   went

7. bring   began

8. begin   took

9. go   became

10. What is a stray animal?

    A. a dangerous animal

    B. a dirty animal

    C. an animal without a home

11. Someone who is persistent

    A. doesn't give up.

    B. is very loud.

    C. can smell very well.

Some sentences can be combined using the word _and_. Use the word _and_ to combine the sentences below. Rewrite them on the lines provided.

12. Our cat smelled gas. He tried to wake us.

    _____

    _____

    _____

81

Predicting Patterns

By studying a given picture, you can determine its **pattern** and predict what will come next.

Study the example above. Then, continue each pattern with three more pictures. Use another sheet of paper if you need more room.

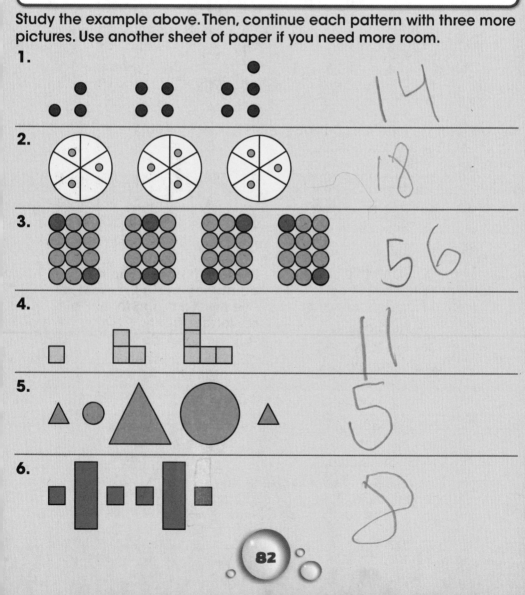

1.

14

2.

18

3.

56

4.

11

5.

5

6.

8

Shapes

> **Parallel lines** run side by side and never cross.
>
> A **quadrilateral** is any shape with four sides.

Study the shapes. Then, answer each question.

square   rectangle   trapezoid   rhombus   circle

triangle   pentagon   hexagon   octagon

1. Which shapes are quadrilaterals?
   rectangle   trapizoid
   square   rhombus

2. Name a quadrilateral with four equal sides. _square_

3. What shape has three sides and three angles? _triangle_

4. What shape has no sides? _circle_

5. What shape has five sides? _pentagon_

6. What shape has six sides? _hexagon_

7. What shape has eight sides? _octogon_

8. What shapes have two or more parallel sides?
   square   octogon
   rectangle   pentagon
   hexagon   trapizod

9. How is a trapezoid different from a rhombus? _One_
   starts with a "t".

Spatial Figures

Spatial figures are solids that take up space. The flat side of a figure is called a **face**.

cube
(6 faces)

sphere

rectangular
prism
(6 faces)

cone
(1 face)

pyramid
(5 faces)

cylinder
(2 faces)

Study the figures above. Then, name the spatial figure that each object looks like. Write the number of faces.

1. cone
1
# of faces

2. cylinder
2
# of faces

3. sphere
0
# of faces

4.
6
# of faces

5. pyramad
5
# of faces

6. cube
6
# of faces

7. cylinder
2
# of faces

8. sphere
0
# of faces

9. pyramid
5
# of faces

10. cone
1
# of faces

11. rectangler prim
6
# of faces

84

Perimeter

The **perimeter (P)** of a figure is the distance around that figure. The perimeter is measured in units, which may be inches, centimeters, miles, or any other unit of measuring length. To find the perimeter, add all of the sides together.

Find the perimeter of each figure. Label your answer in the units shown.

1.

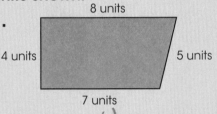

8 units
4 units   5 units
7 units

P = 24

2.

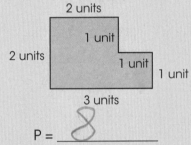

2 units
1 unit
2 units   1 unit
1 unit
3 units

P = 8

3.

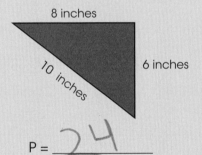

8 inches
10 inches   6 inches

P = 24

4.

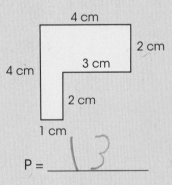

4 cm
2 cm
4 cm   3 cm
2 cm
1 cm

P = 13

5.

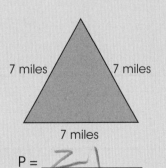

7 miles   7 miles
7 miles

P = 21

6.

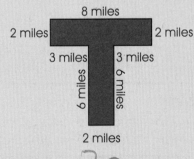

8 miles
2 miles   2 miles
3 miles   3 miles
6 miles   6 miles
2 miles

P = 32

Stamps

Read the passage below. Then, answer the questions.

Some people save stamps. They keep their stamps in albums. They like to look at them. Some people like stamps that are very old. Some people like pretty stamps. Some people like stamps from places that are far away. Some stamps are worth a lot of money. Stamps that were printed incorrectly can be worth the most.

1. Where do some people keep their stamps?

   _____

2. Why do they keep them?

   _____

3. Name two kinds of stamps that people keep.

   _____

4. What kinds of stamps can be worth the most?

   _____

Extra!
Draw a stamp of your own on an envelope. Could you mail a letter with your stamp? Why or why not?

It's All in the Details

Supporting details are the parts of a paragraph that tell more about the topic sentence. They describe the main idea in more detail. The bold phrases below are supporting details.

Jeffrey was having a great day until his mom told him that he had to share his pet snake with his sister. He knew that **Lana would scream and scare his new best friend**. Besides, Lana had been playing dress-up, and **she smelled like a perfume bottle. No pet snake should have to smell like that**.

In each paragraph below, circle the topic sentence and underline two supporting details.

1. Some people like the fire department at the end of our street, and some people do not. My mom and dad think it is great because help could reach us within minutes. Nan's parents do not like it because of all the noise the sirens make. I guess I can see both sides.

2. Every evening, Gabriel and his dad look forward to feeding the deer in their backyard. Gabriel carries the dried corn from the garage to the edge of the woods. He and his dad spread the corn, then hide behind the edge of the house to watch. Each evening, the same four deer come to feed. Maybe someday they will have a newcomer!

3. Allie worked hard to finish all of her projects at summer camp. She tie-dyed her shirt in shades of blue and purple. She glued eyes onto her lion mask. Allie also carefully formed a monkey out of clay. Now, it was time for her favorite camp "project," lunch!

Birds

Read the passage below.

Birds are unique animals. Birds have wings, feathers, and beaks. Birds are the only animals that have feathers. Feathers enable most birds to fly. Their ability to fly helps them stay alive because they can hunt for food, escape their enemies, and migrate away from bad weather. Feathers also protect birds from getting too hot or too cold. Birds have beaks, but they do not have teeth. They use their beaks to get food. Birds eat insects, worms, seeds, and grains.

Birds are protective parents. They lay eggs and build nests to protect their eggs. Usually, the mother bird sits on the nest to keep the eggs warm. Both the mother and father bird keep watch over the nest before the eggs hatch. Nests continue to keep baby birds warm after they hatch from their eggs. Adult birds take care of baby birds until they are ready to fly. They bring food to the baby birds in the nest.

Birds

After reading "Birds," answer the following questions.

1. Circle the sentence that tells the main idea.
    - **A.** Birds are unique animals.
    - **B.** The adult bird teaches its babies how to fly and find food.
    - **C.** Birds are one of the few animals that lay eggs.

Fill in the blanks with the correct answers.

2. Birds are the only animals that have _____ .

3. Birds do not have _____ .

4. Birds lay_____ .

5. Birds build _____ to protect their eggs.

6. Number the sentences in the order that they happen.

    ____ The adult birds bring food to the baby birds in the nest.

    ____ The mother bird sits on the nest to keep the eggs warm.

    ____ Birds build a nest to protect their eggs.

    ____ The adult birds teach their babies how to fly and find food.

7. Write *T* if the sentence is true. Write *F* if the sentence is false.

    ____ All birds can fly.

    ____ Flying helps birds find food.

    ____ Flying protects birds from their enemies.

    ____ Birds migrate to stay away from their enemies.

    ____ Some birds have large teeth.

8. What does *migrate* mean?
    - **A.** to hide under trees
    - **B.** to fly to other places
    - **C.** to find shelter

Action verbs tell what the subject of a sentence does. Circle the action verb in each sentence.

9. Birds fly using their feathers.

10. Birds eat with their beaks instead of teeth.

11. Birds build nests to protect their eggs.

12. Baby birds hatch from eggs.

13. Adult birds bring their baby birds food.

Addition and Subtraction

Problem solving means using the information from a story to solve a math problem.

Example: John ate 12 grapes. Then, he ate 10 more. How many grapes did he eat in all? 12 + 10 = 22, so John ate 22 grapes.

Study the example above. Then, solve each problem.

1. Anthony made 9 clay pots. He broke 4 of the pots. How many pots does he have left?

$9-4=5$

5 clay pots left

2. Keenan had 17 boxes of candy to sell. He sold 2 boxes to his grandma. His dad sold 9 boxes to people at work. How many more boxes did Keenan have to sell?

$9+2=11$

6 more boxes

$\begin{array}{r} 17 \\ -11 \\ \hline 06 \end{array}$

3. Min collects trading cards. She wants to collect all 15 cards in a series. She already has 8 of the cards. How many more cards does Min need?

$15-8=7$

7 more cards in a series

4. Trina had 7 fish in her aquarium. She bought 4 more fish. How many fish does she have altogether?

$7+4=11$ fish

Multiplication

Some word problems can be answered using multiplication. They ask you to find a total number, similar to addition. The difference is that these stories involve equal sets.

Example: Matthew ordered 3 ice cream cones. Each cone had 2 scoops. How many scoops of ice cream did Matthew order?

$$3 \quad \times \quad 2 \quad = \quad 6$$

number of sets   number in each set   total scoops ordered

Study the example above. Then, solve each problem. Show your work.

1. Tina rode her bike 17 miles each day for 6 days. How many miles did Tina ride?

   $17 \times 6 = 102$ miles

2. Jack read 7 books. Each book had 48 pages. How many pages did Jack read?

   $48 \times 7 = 336$ pages

3. Marissa has 5 trading card books. Each book has 50 cards in it. How many trading cards does Marissa have?

   $50 \times 5 = 250$ cards

4. Juan put his stamp collection into 4 boxes. He put 73 stamps in each box. How many stamps does he have?

   $73 \times 4 = 292$ stamps

91

Choosing the Operation

Study the examples on pages 90 and 91. Then, solve each problem.

1. Bev's 3 guinea pigs ate 24 seeds each. How many seeds did the guinea pigs eat?

$8 \times 3 = 24$

8 seeds

2. We found 6 spider webs. Each web had trapped 17 bugs. How many bugs were trapped?

17
17
17
17
17
17

102 bugs

3. A ticket to the game costs $26.00. Amy has $18.00. How much more does Amy need to buy a ticket?

$26.00
-$18.00
0800

800 more ¢
8 more dollars

4. Haley has 52 dimes in her bank. She has 39 nickels. How many coins does she have?

500
+195
695¢

5. We passed 8 trucks on the highway. Each truck honked 4 times. How many honks did the trucks make in all?

$8 \times 4 = 32$

32 honks

6. Jon is making lemonade for 16 people. Each glass needs spoons of powdered mix. How many spoons of powdered mix will Jon use?

$16 \times 2 = 32$ power mix

Page 14: 1. attach; **2.** loud; **3.** cash; **4.** joy; **5.** scatter; **6.** under; **7.** smell; **8.** talk; **9.** mad; **10.** sparkle; **11.** odd; The second car should be circled.

Page 15: Down: **1.** doctor; **2.** smart; **3.** crowd; **4.** grabbed; **5.** bite; **Across:** **6.** remember; **7.** starving; **8.** great

Page 16: expensive/cheap; part/whole; noisy/silent; clean/filthy; toss/catch; safe/dangerous; end/begin; shrink/stretch; child/adult; scared/brave; forget/remember; serious/playful; A Postage Stamp!

Page 17: 1. E.; **2.** F.; **3.** S.; **4.** G.; **5.** A.; **6.** C.; **7.** D.

Page 18: ON HIS FEET!

Page 19: 1. 6,911; **2.** 4,073; **3.** 9,207; **4.** 839; **5.** 9,601; **6.** 8,390; **7.** 417; **8.** 5,082; **9.** 470; **10.** 3,512; **11.** 6,914; **12.** 4,413

Page 20: 1. 1, 3, 4, 5; 1,345; **2.** 2, 1, 6, 1; 2,161; **3.** 1, 0, 3, 0; 1,030; **4.** 3, 1, 0, 0; 3,100; **5.** 2, 4, 4, 0; 2,440; **6.** 1, 2, 1, 3; 1,213

Page 21: 1. 0, 5, 7, 3, 9; **2.** 1, 4, 6, 5, 0; **3.** 2, 7, 3, 8, 1; **4.** 4, 0, 7, 3, 6; **5.** 9, 1, 4, 7, 5; **6.** 5, 5, 8, 3, 7; **7.** 8, 6, 9, 0, 2; **8.** 0, 4, 5, 6, 0; **9.** 3, 1, 0, 4, 8; **10.** 1, 1, 1,

1, 1; **11.** 7, 9, 2, 7, 7; **12.** 6, 8, 5, 9, 3; **13.** 9, 9, 9, 9, 9; **14.** 4, 8, 3, 0, 5; **15.** hundreds, hundreds; **16.** thousands, ten thousands; **17.** ten thousands, tens; **18.** tens, ten thousands; **19.** hundreds, thousands; **20.** ones, tens; **21.** tens, ones; **22.** ten thousands, ten thousands; **23.** thousands, hundreds

Page 22: 1. break; **2.** book; **3.** mean; **4.** tire; **5.** land; **6.** free; **7.** glasses; **8.** straw

Page 23: Answers will vary.

Page 25: 1. C.; **2.** Answers will vary.; **3.** To gulp air to help them stay upright; **4.** A.; **5.** Answers will vary.

Page 26: 1. 9,000 + 5,000 + 10 + 6; **2.** 2,000 + 300 + 50 + 8; **3.** 1,000 + 400 + 0 + 7; **4.** 0 + 900 + 20 + 1; **5.** 7,000 + 800 + 0 + 0; **6.** 3,000 + 200 + 60 + 4; **7.** 5,000 + 100 + 80 + 2; **8.** 0 + 600 + 10 + 4; **9.** 4,000 + 0 + 70 + 3; **10.** 9,000 + 500 + 30 + 0

Page 27: 1. >; **2.** >; **3.** <; **4.** =; **5.** <; **6.** >; **7.** <; **8.** <; **9.** =; **10.** <

Page 28: From left to right and top to bottom: 100, 600, 300, 700, 900, 700, 500, 900

Page 29: 1. 0, 4, 8, 12; **2.** 0, 6, 12; **3.** 33, 36, 39, 42, 45; **4.** 62, 64, 66, 68, 70, 72, 74; **5.** 84, 88, 92, 96

Page 31: 1. A.; **2.** A.; **3.** land/sea; ground/sky; wild/tame; few/many; small/tall; **4.** animals, ants, giraffes, mammals, insects, reptiles, amphibians, cows, birds, trees; **5.** whale; **6.** giraffe; **7.** dog; **8.** snake; **9.** rabbit

Page 33: 1. What Is the Dead Sea?; **2.** The Salty Waters of the Dead Sea; **3.** The Uses of the Dead Sea; **4.** The Water Cycle of the Dead Sea

Page 34: 1. 51, 92, 81, 86, 64; **2.** 94, 130, 92, 92, 103; **3.** 92, 111, 70, 114, 130; **4.** 81, 83, 83, 61, 46; **5.** 70, 62, 96, 90, 81

Page 35: 1. 885, 778, 988, 998, 527; **2.** 594, 986, 969, 789, 919; **3.** 788, 985, 867, 877, 798; **4.** 786, 786, 879, 769, 888; **5.** 985, 678, 899, 957, 898

Page 36: 1. 8,500; 6,712; 9,809; 9,080; 4,401; **2.** 6,308; 13,046; 8,180; 11,055; 9,742; **3.** 8,066; 11,195; 10,191; 9,809; 11,207; **4.** 11,906; 7,600; 7,424; 11,039; 10,889; **5.** 5,008; 10,087; 6,041; 11,817; 11,817

Answer Key

Page 37: 1. $11.37, $12.23; **2.** $13.50, $16.53, $10.58; **3.** $13.34, $18.08, $19.04; **4.** $6.63, $12.70; The left castle is located in the richest kingdom.

Page 38: 1. A.; **2.** B., C.; **3.** B., C., D.

Page 39: (Mammals) Alike: thumb and fingers, drink milk, born alive, similar ears and nose; Different: wings; (Birds) Alike: wings; Different: feathers; Mammal; Answers will vary.

Page 41: 1. The first prince on the left; **2.** T, T, F, F, T; **3.** gentle/men; **4.** horse/shoe; **5.** hand/book; **6.** god/mother; **7.** wrist/watch; **8.** Answers will vary.; **9.** verb: has, subject: shirt, object: buttons; **10.** verb: is wearing, subject: prince, object: crown; **11.** verb: read, subject: Cinderella, object: book; **12.** ugly; **13.** happy, content; **14.** lose; **15.** forget

Page 42: 1. 19, 79, 19, 26, 16; **2.** 19, 58, 14, 59, 28; **3.** 28, 68, 36, 39, 14; **4.** 25, 39, 59, 38, 48; **5.** 38, 29, 49, 8, 58

Page 43: 1. 431, 213, 225, 236, 223; **2.** 553, 322, 812, 121, 205; **3.** 63, 137, 462, 414, 142; **4.** 633, 342, 704, 312, 148; **5.** 220, 414, 260, 316, 541

Page 44: 1. 58, 66, 28, 71, 92; **2.** 24, 59, 19, 81, 32; **3.** 60, 142, 12, 57, 92; **4.** 33, 85, 18, 87, 61; **5.** 39, 47, 19, 92, 89

Page 45: clockwise from the top: 240, 600, 350, 342, 999, 785

Page 46: 1. 3, 3; **2.** 4, 35; **3.** 2, 13; **4.** 6, 57; **5.** 5, 49; **6.** 3, 21; **7.** 3, 3; **8.** 2, 13

Page 47: 1. B.; **2.** B.; **3.** C.; **4.** A.; **5.** B.

Page 49: 1. C.; **2.** C.; **3.** A.; **4.** unify, unicycle; **5.** con/tri/bu/tion; **6.** at/tend/ed; **7.** rep/re/sent/ing; **8.** al/le/giance; **9.** 5, 7–9, 22; **10.** 6, 28–30; **11.** 19, 25

Page 50: 1. 5 + 5 + 5 = 15, 3 x 5 = 15; **2.** 3 + 3 = 6, 2 x 3 = 6; **3.** 2 + 2 + 2 + 2 = 6, 4 x 2 = 8; **4.** 4 + 4 = 8, 2 x 4 = 8; **5.** 3 + 3 + 3 = 9, 3 x 3 = 9; **6.** 4 + 4 + 4 = 12, 3 x 4 = 12; **7.** 2 + 2 + 2 = 6, 3 x 2 = 6; **8.** 5 + 5 = 10, 2 x 5 = 10

Page 51: 1st riddle: YOUR RIGHT ELBOW; 2nd riddle: BECAUSE FISH HAVE THEIR OWN SCALES

Page 52: 1. 48, 22, 26, 39; **3.** 33, 28, 36, 44; **3.** 13, 66, 66, 64; **4.** 84, 48, 44, 63; **5.** 99, 96, 93, 62

Page 53: 1. 90, 70, 91, 72, 110; **2.** 84, 100, 192, 161, 112; **3.** 78, 312, 220, 204, 117; **4.** 252, 270, 288, 112, 56; **5.** 210, 126, 154, 170, 141

Page 54: 1. Birds of Prey; **2.** after; **3.** Wildcat Wackiness, Penguins on Parade; **4.** The Reptile Review; **5.** The Monkey Movie; **6.** Penguin Palace

Page 55: 1. 1, 2, before, now; **2.** 2, 1, soon, immediately; **3.** 1, 2, first, next; **4.** 1, 2, earlier, finally; **5.** 1, 2, right away, eventually; **6.** 2, 1, someday, soon; **7.** 1, 2, eventually, never; **8.** 2, 1, this week, today

Page 56: 1. different; **2.** different; **3.** same; **4.** same; **5.** same; **6.** different; **7.** different; **8.** different; Extra: Answers will vary.

Page 57: Answers will vary.

Page 58: 1. five groups of two circled, 2; **2.** three groups of five circled, 5; **3.** three groups of two circled, 2; **4.** two groups of four circled, 4; **5.** three groups of three circled, 3; **6.** four groups of three circled, 3; **7.** six groups of two circled, 2; **8.** three groups of six circled, 6; **9.** seven groups of two circled, 2

Page 59: All groups in each problem should have the same number of objects drawn. **1.** 3; **2.** 4; **3.** 3; **4.** 4; **5.** 2; **6.** 6

Page 60: 1. 7 r1, 5 r2, 4 r3, 3 r4; **2.** 6 r1, 3 r3, 3 r2, 5 r3; **3.** 7 r7, 9 r1, 5 r1, 4 r4; **4.** 4 r2, 2 r1, 3 r1, 6 r2; **5.** 4 r1, 3 r4, 4 r6, 4 r6

Page 61: 1. 4, 4; **2.** 3, 3; **3.** 4, 4; **4.** 5, 5; **5.** 5, 5; **6.** 3, 3; **7.** 3, 3; **8.** 6, 6; **9.** 5, 5; **10.** 9, 9; **11.** 5, 5; **12.** 2, 2; **13.** 4, 4; **14.** 2, 2; **15.** 6, 6

Page 62: Answers will vary.

Page 65: 1. B.; **2.** C.; **3.** A.; **4.** because they nursed the plant back to health; **5.** because he thought the kids only wanted to visit him to get money

Page 66: 1. 6:30, 11:00, 5:00; **2.** 6:00, 12:30, 10:30

Page 67: 1. 30, 10:00, 10:30; **2.** 15, 2:00, 2:15; **3.** 35, 7:00, 7:35; **4.** 55, 9:00, 9:55; **5.** 10, 8:00, 8:10; **6.** 50, 4:00, 4:50; **7.** 5, 10:00, 10:05; **8.** 45, 6:00, 6:45

Page 68: 1. $1.55; **2.** $2.48; **3.** $7.45; **4.** $10.85; **5.** $17.17; **6.** $33.22

Page 69: 1. $3.90; **2.** $3.80; **3.** $4.05;

4. $5.40; **5.** $0.50; **6.** $4.05; **7.** $0.85; **8.** $15.00; **9.** $0.81; **10.** $0.05

Page 71: 1. B.; **2.** C.; **3.–6.** Answers will vary. **7.** warm, warmest; **8.** happy, happiest; **9.** short, shortest; **10.** old, oldest; **11.** high, highest; **12.** because it was too warm in spring and the snow would melt; **13.** showers, sun warming the earth; **14.** shorter days, longer nights, crisp, cool air

Page 72: 1. B.; **2.** A.; **3.** C.

Page 73: Answers will vary.

Page 74: 1. $\frac{1}{6}$; **2.** $\frac{3}{8}$; **3.** $\frac{3}{4}$; **4.** $\frac{5}{8}$; **5.** $\frac{7}{9}$; **6.** $\frac{7}{12}$

Page 75: 1. 2, 3, 12, 15; **2.** 2, 3, 16, 5; **3.** 4, 9, 8, 15; **4.** 8, 12, Answers will vary; **5.** 8, 9, 28, 28

Page 76: blue: 0.8, 0.1, 0.7, 0.6, 0.4, 0.9; green: 0.15, 0.73, 0.36, 0.81

Page 77: 1. 1, 0, 7; **2.** 5, 6, 0; **3.** 3, 9, 1; **4.** 16, 0, 6; **5.** 0, 1, 3; **6.** 7, 9, 3; **7.** 3, 0, 1; **8.** 1, 2, 5; **9.** 4, 1, 1; **10.** 2, 5, 3; **11.** 9, 1, 0; **12.** 8, 8, 4;

13. 1.80

14. 3.2

15. 4.2

16. 3.07

17. 4.23

Page 79: 1. B.; **2.** C.; **3.** A.; **4.** B.; **5.** Answers will vary.

Page 81: 1. 1, 6, 2, 3, 4, 5; **2.** B.; **3.** C.; **4.** C.; **5.** take/took; **6.** become/became; **7.** bring/brought; **8.** begin/began; **9.** go/went; **10.** C.; **11.** A.; **12.** Our cat smelled gas and tried to wake us.

Page 82:

1.

2.

3.

4.

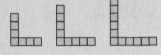

5.

6.

Page 83: 1. square, rhombus, rectangle, trapezoid; **2.** square or rhombus; **3.** triangle; **4.** circle; **5.** pentagon; **6.** hexagon; **7.** octagon; **8.** square, rhombus, rectangle, hexagon, trapezoid, octagon; **9.** Answers will vary but may include a trapezoid has one pair of parallel sides, but a rhombus has two pairs of parallel sides.

Page 84: 1. cone, 1; **2.** cylinder, 2; **3.** sphere, 0; **4.** rectangular prism, 6; **5.** pyramid, 5; **6.** cube, 6; **7.** cylinder, 2; **8.** sphere, 0; **9.** pyramid, 5; **10.** cone, 1; **11.** rectangular prism, 6

Page 85: 1. 24 units; **2.** 10 units; **3.** 24 inches; **4.** 16 cm; **5.** 21 miles; **6.** 32 miles

Page 86: 1. in albums; **2.** because they like to look at them; **3.** old, pretty, stamps from far away places; **4.** stamps that were printed incorrectly; Extra: Answers will vary.; No, because a stamp must be from a government post office to mail a letter.

Page 87: 1. Topic Sentence: Some people like the fire department at the end of our street, and some people do not.; Supporting Details: My mom and dad think it is great because help could reach us within minutes. Nan's parents do not like it because of all the noise the sirens make.; **2.** Topic Sentence: Every evening, Gabriel and his dad look forward to feeding the deer in the backyard.; Supporting Details: Gabriel carries the dried corn from the garage to the edge of the woods. He and his dad spread the corn, then hide behind the edge of the house to watch.; **3.** Topic Sentence: Allie worked hard to finish all of her projects at summer camp.; Supporting Details: She tie-dyed her shirt in shades of blue and purple. She glued eyes onto her lion's mask.

Page 89: 1. A.; **2.** feathers; **3.** teeth; **4.** eggs; **5.** nests; **6.** 3, 2, 1, 4; **7.** F, T, T, F, F; **8.** B.; **9.** fly; **10.** eat; **11.** build; **12.** hatch; **13.** bring

Page 90: 1. 5 pots; **2.** 6 boxes; **3.** 7 cards; **4.** 11 fish

Page 91: 1. 102 miles; **2.** 336 pages; **3.** 250 trading cards; **4.** 292 stamps

Page 92: 1. 72 seeds; **2.** 102 bugs; **3.** $8.00; **4.** 91 coins; **5.** 32 honks; **6.** 48 spoons of powdered mix